Route 66

Route 66

MAIN STREET USA

Nick Freeth

MBI Publishing Company

EDITOR: **Philip de Ste. Croix**
DESIGNER: **Philip Clucas** MSIAD
PHOTOGRAPHER: **Neil Sutherland**
COMMISSIONING EDITOR: **Will Steeds**
PRODUCTION: **Phillip Chamberlain**
INDEX: **Amanda O'Neill**
COLOR REPRODUCTION: **Media Print (UK) Limited**
PRINTED AND BOUND in Spain

About the author:
Nick Freeth was born in London in 1956, and is a graduate of Cambridge University. He spent 12 years as a staffer at the BBC World Service, where he specialized in music radio production, and has subsequently worked in commercial broadcasting and as a freelance audio producer. Nick has a long-standing fascination with American culture: he is the co-author of three successful books focusing on the development of the guitar in the USA, and in 2001 his illustrated guide *Traveling Route 66* was published by Oklahoma University Press.

This edition first published in 2001 by
MBI Publishing Company,
Galtier Plaza, Suite 200
380 Jackson Street
St. Paul, MN   55101-3885

Produced by Salamander Books Ltd.,
8, Blenheim Court, Brewery Road,
London N7 9NY, United Kingdom

© 2001 Salamander Books Ltd

A member of the Chrysalis Group plc

MBI Publishing Company books are also available at discounts in bulk quantity for industrial or sales-promotional use. For details write to Special Sales Manager at Motorbooks International Wholesalers & Distributors, Galtier Plaza, Suite 200, 380 Jackson Street, St. Paul, MN 55101-3885.

Library of Congress Cataloging-in-Publication Data Available.

ISBN 0-7603-0864-0

R · O · U · T · E   6 · 6

CONTENTS

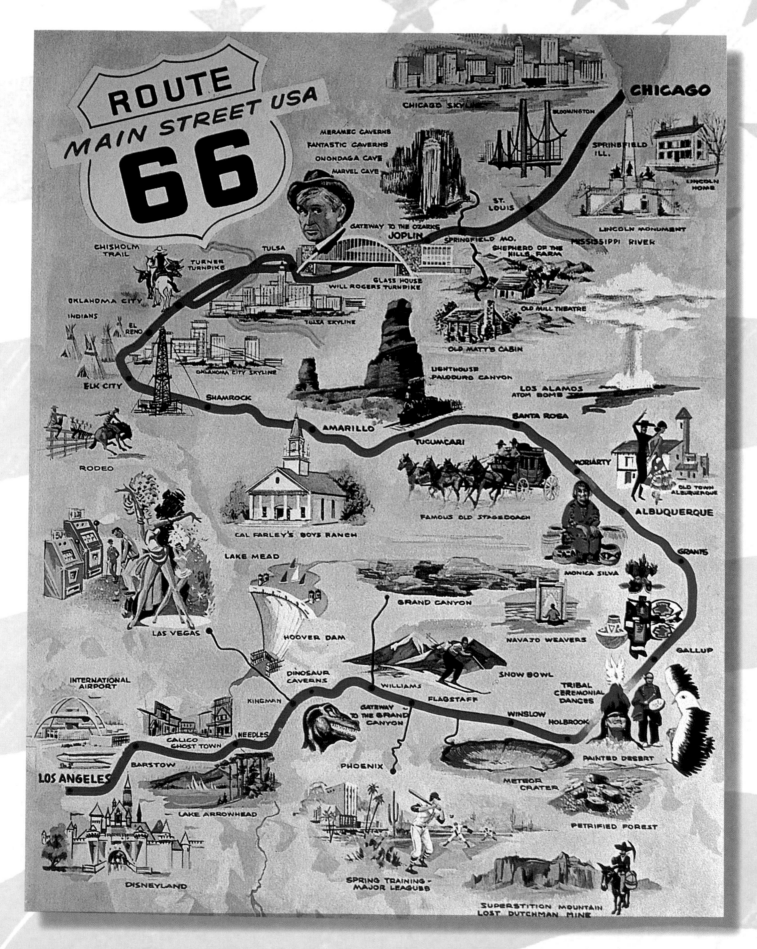

Foreword

Route 66, with undisputed certainty, reigns as the most storied highway in the United States. A recurring theme in American literature, Route 66 has been the star of more stories, books, songs, movies, and television shows than any other highway in the United States. The road is more popular than Route 1 – running from Maine to Keywest, Florida. From the mid-1920s, Route 66 was more traveled than Highway 101 on the Pacific coast, and better known than the Pennsylvania Turnpike or the Alcan Highway.

Route 66 came closer than any other highway to becoming the National Road. And in the halcyon days of US 66, it became the most magical road in all the world. A legend was in the making.

And what a legend it would be.

National magazines called Route 66 "America's worst speed trap," naming the tiny towns where cops and judges had their palms outstretched for bribes. The American Automobile Association reported on towns that should be avoided, unless drivers were prepared to sweeten the police treasury. In the Roaring Twenties, desperadoes and bootleggers – the likes of John Dillinger, Al Capone, Bugs Moran, Pretty Boy Floyd, Bonnie and Clyde, and Ma Barker and her god-fearing boys lurched down Old 66, using it as an escape route.

Above: Much of 66 is well-maintained and smooth surfaced – but there are some rougher sections, like this stretch of road near Jericho Gap, Texas, which dead ends as a muddy track.

The road was a highway of flat tires, water bags hanging on the car radiator, motor courts, evaporator coolers in the car window, tourist traps, treacherous curves, narrow lanes, and detour signs. Route 66 was Wolfman Jack on all-night radio, convoy trucks, the Bunion Derby, Continental Trailways, and Greyhound buses, free road maps and coloring books for the kids, family reunions, 25¢ haircuts, a 5¢ cup of coffee, Burma Shave jingles, and wooden billboards that promised "Tucumcari Tonight." Folks guzzled Grape Ne-Hi soda pop, and hitchhiking was safe.

Through good times and hard times, the highway became a symbol of faith for the future. Novelist John Steinbeck set the tone of the road in his Pulitzer Prize book, *The Grapes of Wrath,* when he found a nurturing quality of the highway and called Route 66 "The Mother Road." It was a "Road of second chance" and the "Glory Road" to the immigrants of the dust bowl. And to travel agencies it was the chosen thoroughfare for the growing numbers of discriminating American tourists.

Left: "It winds from Chicago to L.A..." – an illustrated map of Route 66,
showing its cities and sights, and also suggesting some side trips – including visits
to the Grand Canyon and Las Vegas!

Route 66 was to carry a sundry of names at different locations throughout her history – names like The Pontiac Trail, Osage Indian Trail, Wire Road, Postal Highway, Grand Canyon Route, National Old Trails Highway, Ozark Trail, Will Rogers Highway, and because it went through the center of so many towns, the highway became known as The Main Street of America.

Singer, composer Bobby Troup's bluesy, musical hit of 1946, "Route 66," celebrated the end of World War II, and gas and food rationing. Originally crooned by Nat "King" Cole and belted out by the Andrews Sisters, the simple tune became a highway national anthem. Nothing captured America's love affair with the road more than this song. Millions of motoring adventurers, addicted to the smell of gasoline and the drone of rubber on the pavement, took Bobby's suggestion to heart and plotted a course that would take them on a vacation across U.S. Highway 66.

Above: "Family on the Road," a famous photograph taken by Dorothea Lange (1895–1965) during the mass exodus from the Oklahoma dustbowl in the 1930s.

The 1950s saw Route 66 reach genuine celebrity status. Families could leave their homes in the East and Midwest and drive to the Painted Desert or The Grand Canyon. They could drive all the way to the Pacific Ocean on a highway that passed through towns where the young outlaw Jesse James robbed banks; where Abraham Lincoln practiced law; and cross the great river Mark Twain wrote about. Tourists could see snake pits and caged, wild critters, and real live cowboys and Indians.

Route 66 reached even greater popularity during 1960–64 when a nomadic pot boiler by the same name as the highway became a popular TV show. "route 66" (yes, the "r" was not capitalized in the show's title) was the story of two young adventurers, Buz (George Maharis) and Tod (Martin Milner), getting their kicks on Route 66 in a Corvette. The show established the Corvette as a national icon and sold more 'vettes than any other Chevrolet advertising or promotion since.

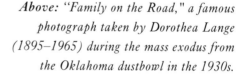

Above: Part of Ella's Frontier, an abandoned and now largely demolished trading post near Joseph City, Arizona.

When the Federal Highway Act of 1956 called for the construction of Interstate systems throughout the United States, it looked as if the bright lights of fame and fortune that had shined on Route 66 for so many years was beginning to dim. Little by little, here and there, pieces of The Mother Road was replaced by the interstates.

Bypassing of towns that the fabled highway had served was a task that took five different super highways to achieve – Interstate 55 from Chicago to St. Louis, Interstate 44 from St. Louis to Oklahoma City, Interstate 40 from Oklahoma City to Barstow, Interstate 15 from Barstow to San Bernardino, and Interstate 10 from San Bernardino to Santa Monica. The last stretch of Route 66 was bypassed by Interstate 40 in 1984 at Williams, Arizona. There was a ceremony, almost a wake. The late Bobby Troup called the occasion "a very sad day."

Because Route 66 was decertified in 1985 and no longer is classified as a Federal Highway, some folks will tell you the road is no longer there. But progress does not necessarily conquer all. Beyond the blandness of the Interstates, the fast food chains, and the smell of diesel fumes, is a powerful rhythm of an old two-lane ribbon of asphalt and concrete that still rises and twists and turns across rolling hills, the mountains, and the deserts. Slowing through quiet towns, then rushing on and up again to the next ridge, you'll find the road waiting to be discovered in each of the eight Route 66 states.

Above: "(Get Your Kicks on) Route 66", written by Bobby Troup (1918-1999) in 1946, has subsequently been recorded by more than 130 different artists.

Roadside attractions have been revived, restored, and reopened along the fabled highway. Folks in classic cars cruise into a drive-in for a hamburger and shake. Service station attendants offer to check under the hood and wash the windshield. Family-owned restaurants serve blue-plate specials. A waitress in a starched pink uniform calls you "Hon," and a vintage Wurlitzer jukebox blares out "Good Night Irene." The old road still beckons pilgrims not only from across America, but people from every compass point of the world.

With the car open to the wind, and the radio tuned to an AM station riddled with static from a thunderstorm on the horizon, memories flicker in the sweetness of the moment. The miles themselves dissolve every question except the one that matters. What lies waiting, there, just over the rise of Route 66?

Paul Taylor
Publisher, *Route 66 Magazine*

Left: All along Route 66, jukeboxes play the music of the road.

Introduction

Below: A photograph from the collection of Nate Skokusen Jr., whose father's road contracting company built substantial sections of Route 66 in New Mexico and Arizona.

Bottom: Engineers' field book, chalk, and marking stake (labeled "66+66").

On May 10, 1869, the first intercontinental railroad in the USA, linking New York to San Francisco, was completed when tracks laid by the Union Pacific and Central Pacific companies came together at Promontory Point, Utah. It was now possible to travel from coast to coast in just a few days; and the railroad networks' continuing expansion over the following decades made long-distance transportation – often uncomfortable, expensive, and even hazardous in the pre-rail era – relatively cheap and practicable for passengers, mail, and freight. Thanks to trains, the American dream of "uniting the continent in fact as well as in sentiment and political theory" (in the words of journalist and historian Alistair Cooke) was rapidly becoming a reality.

But railroads could not reach everywhere, and the contrast between their huge subsidies and the chronic under-investment in America's highways was revealed in statistics published by the U.S. Office of Road Inquiry in 1904. They showed that more than 90 percent of the 2,000,000-odd miles of the nation's roads and trails were still dirt surfaced, sometimes impassable in bad weather, and clearly inadequate for the newly dawning age of the automobile.

Pressure for highway improvement grew steadily in the years before World War I. At first, as Susan Croce Kelly explains in her study of *Route 66: The*

Above: Another powerful photo of 1930s dustbowl migrants on 66 taken by Dorothea Lange for the Farm Security Amdinistration.

Highway and its People, road building "was a local venture and roads [like the Ozark Trail or Old Wire Road] were marked and maintained by booster groups supported through individual donations." But the so-called "good roads" movement also spawned some more ambitious ideas, among them a

proposal for the construction of a gravel-surfaced thoroughfare between New York and San Francisco. The Lincoln Highway, as it was named, was America's first long-distance road project; its development and the problems it encountered were to have a significant effect on all subsequent highway planning.

The prime mover behind the Lincoln Highway was Carl G. Fisher, founder of automobile headlight manufacturer Prest-O-Lite. His contacts in the motor industry, coupled with his fund-raising skills and genius for publicity, created an impressive level of support for the New York-San Francisco road. A group of industrialists donated $4,000,000 towards it, while thousands of private individuals underwrote the venture by purchasing annual "Highway Memberships" costing $5 or $100. In October 1913, after a year of tireless promotion by its backers (who even persuaded President Woodrow Wilson to subscribe to the project) the Lincoln Highway was formally commissioned.

However, it became clear that the huge sums needed to surface its 3389 mile (5457km) length could not be raised by private enterprise. The route

Below: Part of the road to Albuquerque from Santa Fe – an alignment used by Route 66 until 1937.
Below, center: A rest stop by the roadside for an elegant early user of Route 66.

ON THE NATIONAL OLD TRAILS HIGHWAY — OCEAN TO OCEAN

HAIR-PIN CURVE, NATIONAL OLD TRAILS HIGHWAY, BETWEEN KINGMAN AND OATMAN, ARIZONA

Above: The old road leading over the Sitgreaves Pass and down to Oatman, Arizona – another potentially hazardous section of highway.
Left: A truck at Landergin, a railroad work camp between Vega and Adrian, Texas.

remained largely unpaved and inadequately marked for years afterwards; in 1923, the Bureau of Public Roads assumed responsibility for its completion, and eventually, the Lincoln Highway lost its identity when it was incorporated into the numbered US road system.

Above: A second vintage postcard view of La Bajada Hill, New Mexico. This twisting road, with its steep gradient, would have posed a severe challenge for many vehicles.

Below: Anxieties about 66's future grew in the years following World War II, as the Old Road's increasing congestion led some travelers to seek out other routes for their east-west journeys.

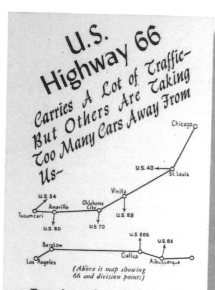

The Lincoln episode demonstrated that large-scale road planning and construction was the business of state and government authorities, not individual entrepreneurs. Co-ordination and regulation were required to ensure that highways were properly signposted and maintained, and an overhaul of the existing network was needed to bring about the improvements demanded by increasing levels of automobile ownership and mobility. After representations from the American Association of State Highway Officials in 1924, the US Secretary of Agriculture decided to delegate the task of reorganizing the nation's roads to a specially convened committee of experts. Among them was Cyrus Stevens Avery (1871–1962), born in Pennsylvania but a long-time resident of Tulsa, Oklahoma, who had been a highway commissioner in his adopted home state for over a decade, and was soon to become nationally famous as the "Father of Route 66."

After their first meeting in Spring 1925, Cyrus Avery and his colleagues launched a scheme to replace the old trails network with a numbered, clearly signposted system of national highways. These "routes" were to be based on existing roads, and federal aid would be provided to upgrade and widen them. One of the most significant routes to be defined and developed by the officials over the following months was the key east-west thoroughfare from Chicago to Los Angeles, to which Avery originally assigned the number 60 (zero suffixes were reserved for major highways). At this stage, the newly conceived road was still largely inadequate for heavy traffic. Concreting was well advanced on its eastern section, but elsewhere, the highway was surfaced with mud or dirt, while in a few desert areas there was no road bed at all – only wooden planks for vehicles to drive along. It took years of strenuous work (much of it done with

Right: Route 66 passing through the center of Winslow, Arizona. Many communities on the path of the Old Road were dependent on the business it brought to their doors - and some never recovered from its decommissioning.

primitive, mule-driven construction gear) to bring the Illinois-California route to the required standard; in some states, paving was not fully completed until the mid-1930s.

There was also considerable controversy over the path the new road should take. Some lobbyists wanted 60 to head to California via Colorado, Utah, and Nevada; but Avery, determined that it should pass through Oklahoma, succeeded in obtaining the more southerly route he favored. By October 1925, the highway's basic direction – from Chicago via Missouri, Kansas, Oklahoma, Texas, New Mexico, and Arizona to California – had been agreed. However, Avery did not get his way over its numbering. "60" was eventually allocated to the route between Missouri and the Virginia coast, while the Chicago-L.A. thoroughfare was named 66. It was officially commissioned, with the other new roads planned by the committee, in November 1926.

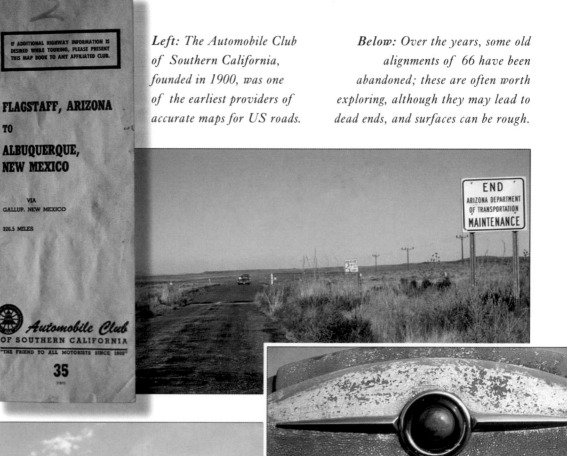

Left: The Automobile Club of Southern California, founded in 1900, was one of the earliest providers of accurate maps for US roads.

Below: Over the years, some old alignments of 66 have been abandoned; these are often worth exploring, although they may lead to dead ends, and surfaces can be rough.

Above: The ruins and disused machinery found by the roadside of Route 66 are an intrinsic part of its unique atmosphere.

Left: The El Morro National Monument lies southwest of Route 66 in the Malpais region of New Mexico, and is one of the many remarkable sites worth taking a side-trip to visit.

ROUTE 66

Illinois

From its starting point in downtown Chicago, Route 66 heads southwest across the prairies to the state capital, Springfield, and on toward the low-lying plains around the Mississippi River, which forms the border with Missouri. The highway runs close to its modern counterpart, I-55, and there are also frequent glimpses of the railroad – the original east-west thoroughfare that brought Illinois so much of its wealth and importance.

Main picture: At the start of Route 66 – looking west down Chicago's Jackson Drive from Lake Shore Drive during the morning rush hour.
Above: Dell Rhea Chicken Basket at 79th and Old Route 66, Willowbrook, a few miles outside Chicago – a long-established eatery famous for top-class live entertainment as well as good food.

Illinois

Below: Route 66 travelers are unlikely to go hungry in Illinois. Establishments like the Luna Café, near Mitchell, have many years' experience of providing food and drink for motorists, and their garish roadside markers are now landmarks in their own right. Perhaps the most striking of these is the Gemini Giant (right) outside the Launching Pad Café in Wilmington.

By the mid-19th century, Chicago was already a significant commercial center with impressive local and long distance transportation links. In 1836, construction had started on its first railroad, the Galena and Chicago Union, linking it to an important lead-mining settlement about 140 miles (225km) to the northwest. The line was opened in 1848, and in the same year the Illinois and Michigan Canal was completed – helping to establish the city as a major inland port.

Later, the region's attitude to highway development was similarly energetic and far-sighted. There was considerable support within Illinois for the "Good Roads" movement, a pressure group started in the early 1900s by vehicle manufacturers and automobile clubs, which was instrumental in gaining public funding for highway building. In 1921, work began on a federally financed, fully paved 295-mile (475km) road between Chicago and East St. Louis. This was finished five years later, and almost immediately became part of Route 66, which had been commissioned just months before; at the time, the only other properly surfaced stretch of the new east-west highway nearing completion was in Kansas.

Over the years, there have been a number of minor alterations to 66's path through Illinois. Its starting point, originally at the intersection of Chicago's Jackson Boulevard and Michigan Avenue, has been moved twice: first, in the 1930s, to Jackson and Lake Shore Drive (near Grant Park), and later to the junction of Adams and Michigan. In 1940, its Joliet section, about 40 miles (64km) southwest of the city (described on pages 18-19) was designated an "alternate" route, and the main highway was diverted via Plainfield – a less interesting alignment

Below: Route 66's guardians of law and order: two Illinois state policemen, photographed in the 1940s.

STEAKS CHICKEN SEA FOOD *Luna* CAFE

fine drinks pkg. goods

that eventually rejoined the Old Road at Braidwood. Another early segment of 66 beyond Springfield was abandoned in 1930; this change, which bypassed several smaller settlements, is explained in more detail on pages 30–31.

Navigating through Illinois on Route 66 is comparatively straightforward: except in downtown Chicago, the highway is well signposted, and a very high proportion of it can be driven without recourse to the Interstate. Surfaces are generally good; in fact, 66 often offers a smoother ride than I-55, which is constantly assailed by heavy traffic. Perhaps the only word of warning should be to travelers who are unfamiliar with Chicago: the "Windy City" certainly lives up to its name!

Below: Interstate 55, Route 66 and the railroad running in parallel west of Gardiner.

Above: The Harriet Dean House in downtown Springfield, just across the street from Abraham Lincoln's home. This area of the city has been restored by the U.S. National Park Service.

Below: Matchbooks like these were widely used to promote local businesses.

Below: The facilities offered by this YMCA hotel in Chicago seem basic by today's standards – but early travelers on Route 66 could expect to find much less luxurious accommodation outside the big cities. It took several decades for the modern motel to evolve from its more spartan predecessors, the motor camp and tourist court.

Chicago owes its existence to trade and transportation, and the creation of Route 66 in 1926 added a reliable long-distance road link to its existing shipping and rail systems. Today, the city seems as busy and restless as ever; but Interstate 55 now provides the main path for its endless westward traffic, and the start of 66, at the junction of Adams and Michigan, is poorly marked and easy to miss. The first sense of actually being on the Old Road comes after turning onto Ogden Avenue. Here, the "historic Route 66" markers begin to appear, as the highway leads through the districts of Cicero (famous for its links with Chicago's most notorious gangster, Al Capone, whose criminal activities led Cicero to be nicknamed "Syndicate City" in the mid-1920s) and Berwyn, and then via Harlem Avenue (SR 43) and Joliet Road to I-55.

At Willowbrook, near the Interstate's junction with SR 83, is a Route 66 institution – Dell Rhea's Chicken Basket. First opened in the

Above: Chicago's majestic Union Station is sited on Jackson Boulevard; this photograph shows its Clinton Street facade. It dates from 1925, when railroads were still America's prime provider of long distance transportation .

GUEST ROOMS AT THE Y.M.C.A. HOTEL — CHICAGO

* BOBBY TROUP * 1946 * LONDONTOWN MUSIC *

IF YOU EVER PLAN TO MOTOR WEST: TRAVEL MY WAY, TAKE THE HIGHWAY THAT'S THE BEST. *GET YOUR KICKS ON ROUTE 66!* IT WINDS FROM CHICAGO TO L.A., MORE THAN 2,000 MILES ALL THE WAY. *GET YOUR KICKS ON ROUTE 66!* NOW YOU GO THRU ST. LOOEY... JOPLIN, MISSOURI! AND OKLAHOMA CITY LOOKS MIGHTY PRETTY. YOU'LL SEE AMARILLO... GALLUP, NEW MEXICO. FLAGSTAFF, ARIZONA: DON'T FORGET WINONA, KINGMAN, BARSTOW, SAN BERNARDINO. WON'T YOU... GET HIP TO THIS TIMELY TIP: WHEN YOU... MAKE THAT CALIFORNIA TRIP: *GET YOUR KICKS ON ROUTE 66!*

ROUTE US 66

© 1996 H.Sperl

LPS 569

7N9S9UR3

| 0099 | Chenoa | 0118 | Towanda | 0137 | Funks Grove | 0152 | Lincoln | 0177 |
| Pontiac | 0108 | Lexington | 0126 | Normal/Bloomington | 0147 | McLean | 0167 | Broadwell |

> ❝ **It winds from Chicago to L.A.,**
> **More than two thousand miles all the way.**
> **Get your kicks on Route Sixty-Six!** ❞
>
> *from "Route 66" by Bobby Troup, 1946*

1930s as a gas station with a lunch counter, it later became a restaurant with a reputation for fine live blues music, featuring top performers such as singer Koko Taylor. Today, it continues to provide excellent food and entertainment, and also houses an impressive collection of 66 memorabilia.

To follow the Old Road's original alignment, turn off onto SR 53 near Bollingbrook, a few miles

Above: Heading away from Chicago down Joliet Road. The Old Road is easy to follow in this area thanks to the distinctive "Historic Route 66" signs.

Right: Looking east from just beyond Elwood – one of the many locations along the way where Route 66 runs close to the railroad tracks.
Far left: The theme song of the Old Road – Bobby Troup's classic "(Get Your Kicks On) Route 66."

southwest of Dell Rhea's, and head towards Joliet. Outside the town lies the Stateville Penitentiary, immortalized by John Belushi and Dan Aykroyd's 1980 movie, *The Blues Brothers*. In real life, the prison is best viewed from the highway; casual visitors are turned away at the gates and forbidden to photograph its striking façade. Beyond Joliet – home of the 66 Speedway racetracks, opened in 1998 – Route 66 stretches southwest to Elwood and beyond.

Below: Any time is a good time to stop at Braidwood's Polk-a-Dot Drive In... This outdoor clock face features the distinctive color scheme used by the famous eatery since its earliest days. In the words of the restaurant's celebrated slogan, "If you're not at the Dot, you're not cruisin'!"

Wilmington, on SR 53 as it follows the path of Route 66 southwest from Elwood, is most famous for its "Gemini Giant:" a 20-foot (6m) fiberglass spaceman who stands by the roadside outside the town's Launching Pad Café. The Giant, one of three similar statues made for Illinois businesses by a Californian company, has been attracting attention and customers since the Launching Pad first opened in the early 1960s; the café's menu combines standard road fare with novelties such as Pina Colada milkshakes!

About five miles (8km) further down the highway lies another remarkable restaurant: Braidwood's Polk-a-Dot Drive-In, which dates back to the 1950s. This started out as a mobile kitchen installed in an old school bus painted with rainbow polka dots, and retained its distinctive color

Above: Odell's Sinclair gas station, dating from 1932, and currrently under restoration thanks to efforts by local citizens and conservationists

scheme after moving to its current premises. Since 1996, the Polk-a-Dot has hosted an annual 66 "Cruise Nite," featuring road-related awards, prizes, and music.

Left: The Gemini Giant looming over Wilmington's Launching Pad Drive-In. The 20-foot (6m) spaceman has attracted thousands of customers to this popular roadside diner.

Below: The Giant stands on the right of Route 66 as it heads southwest through Elwood. To his left (out of shot) lies the Launching Pad Drive-In; directly behind him is a private house. Since the advent of I-55, the Old Road is much quieter.

Across the flat landscape between Braidwood and Gardner, 66 runs parallel to the railroad and I-55; south of Gardner, it becomes a frontage road alongside the Interstate (follow the "Route 66" signs to keep on track). Outside major cities, main highways often stay close to the Old Road, while bypassing the small towns and settlements that give it so much of its character. Travelers on 66 are free to enjoy these at a more leisurely pace, and are rewarded by glimpses of remnants from an earlier, more picturesque era of American motoring – like the two memorable gas stations at Dwight and Odell, both opened in the early 1930s. The Dwight station was a Marathon Oil outlet, while the one at Odell was originally operated by Standard and subsequently run by Phillips 66 and Sinclair. It is currently being restored as part of a tourism and community development project by the citizens of Odell.

Eateries

Opposite (clockwise from top left): *Pop Hicks Restaurant in Clinton, OK; a menu with a personal greeting by the owner who gave it his name, Ethan A. Hicks (he acquired the nickname "Pop" from one of his waitresses); the interior of the eatery (probably photographed in the 1940s); the Waldmire family's Cozy Drive In, Springfield, IL; a flyer for the long-defunct Mr. Arky Barbeque on Foothill Boulevard, Fontana, CA; a postcard showing Ben Stanley's Café in Miami, OK – its famous slogan was "We don't fool you, we feed you;" and a view of another Old Road favorite, Dowell's Saratoga Café in Amarillo, TX.*

Many of the earliest suppliers of food on Route 66 started out selling gas before diversifying into snacks and drinks. As Michael Karl Witzel explains in his book *Route 66 Remembered*, "The petroleum peddlers of the 1920s began to view 'edible' fuel as just another aspect of car commerce. With underfed travelers already parked at the pumps, it was only good business to provide them with the victuals they desired." Menus concentrated on what was quick to prepare and easy to consume either on the premises or on the move: sandwiches, soft drinks, coffee, and basic cooked foods like pies, hamburgers, and hot dogs.

As the volume of traffic (and potential business) increased, Route 66's caterers became more adventurous and enterprising. Roadside stands, diners and drive-ins flourished, most of them small, family-run concerns. But larger franchises and chains were soon competing with them, including companies like White Castle – the pioneer of many supply and marketing methods that later became standard fast food practice. In 1931, White Castle was the first firm to deliver hamburger patties to its outlets deep frozen; the following year it launched a revolutionary (and widely copied) coupon campaign, offering five burgers for the price of two.

Some individual restaurateurs on 66 later became "big boys" themselves: Gus Belt's "Steak 'n Shake" empire developed from a single diner in Normal, Illinois; and "Chicken in the Rough," a poultry dish created in 1937 by Beverly and Rubye Osborne at their Oklahoma City eatery, was franchised to scores of other restaurants from Chicago to Los Angeles. But the biggest success story in Route 66 catering was that of Dick and Maurice McDonald, whose "Speedee Service System," introduced at the brothers' San Bernadino premises in December 1948, revolutionized the roadside food business, and formed the basis for their burger chain's eventual global dominance.

"Good Morning"

Pop Hicks "on 66"

We appreciate your patronage and hope we may continue to merit it. If we please you, tell your friends. If we don't, tell us. We strive to satisfy.

Pop Hicks

HAM AND EGGS	SAUSAGE AND EGGS	BACON AND EGGS
TOAST, JELLY, COFFEE	TOAST, JELLY, COFFEE	TOAST, JELLY, COFFEE
95¢	85¢	85¢

Fruits and Juices

Prune Juice .... .15 & .25   Orange Juice (Small) .... .15
Grapefruit Half .... .35   Orange Juice (Large) .... .25
Grapefruit Juice (Small) .... .15   Prunes .... .25
Grapefruit Juice (Large) .... .25   Tomato Juice (Small) .... .15

Fresh, Crisp Cereals

With Milk .... .30   With Half and Half .... .35

Kellogg's Corn Flakes   Pop   Shredded Wheat
Al-Bran   Sugar Corn Pops   Rice Krispies
Kellogg's 40% Bran Flakes   Sugar Frosted Flakes
Kellogg's Raisin Bran   Custard Cereal

From our Grill

Fresh Eggs (2) Any Style, Coffee ....
One Egg, Toast, Coffee ....
Three Hot Cakes with Syrup, Coffee ....
Two Hot Cakes with Syrup, Coffee ....
Waffle with Syrup, Coffee ....
Side Order Bacon ....
Side Order Sausage ....
Side Order Ham ....
Plain Omelet ....
With Jelly or Cheese ....

Pastries and Toast

SWEET ROLL .... .10   TOAST ....
DOUGHNUTS .... .10   FRENCH TOAST .... .30

POP HICKS RESTAURANT — Hiway 66 — Clinton, Okla.

OOZY DOGS

Ben Stanley's CAFE
Nationally Famous
STEAKS
CHICKEN
SEA FOOD
One Mile South of
MIAMI, OKLA.
on Hi-way 66

"MR. ARKY SAYS-"MARY HAD A LITTLE LAMB, WE ALL KNOW THAT ..... NOW YOU SEE WHAT WE HAVE!"

COME IN WE GOT THE FOOD BUT OUT OF CASH

SWIPED FROM

MR. ARKY BARBEQUE

Gone ARKANSAS FOR A LOAD OF HICKORY WOOD

See you TUESDAY Mr. ARKY is TIRED

"NEW GOODS ARRIVING DAILY ...WHAT'S NEW WE SHOW"

We know a fellow with a jolly good laugh
Who will roast you a sandwich from the leg of a calf
He will toast it well done not one bit raw
And it's flavored with hickory from old Ark-an-saw

He is on highway 66 just out from town
Drive out for a barbecue sandwich tasty and brown
It's from over the Desert and out of the draw
And it's smoked in hickory from old Ark-an-saw

OPEN

HIGHWAY 66, FONTANA · · · TELEPHONE 9468 · · WE CLOSE EVERY SUMMER ON ACCOUNT OF GOOD HEALTH

Below: The exit for Funks Grove, whose maple trees supply sap for the Funk family's delicious maple sirup. The area is one of the very few sirup-producing centers in this part of America; most commercial maple groves lie well to the north.

Right: Two alignments of 66 near Lexington: on the left is an old, abandoned pavement, replaced by the single-lane carriageway to its right.

Above: A roadside shield outside Towanda provides information about the Old Road. It was erected by one of the many associations dedicated to preserving and promoting the highway.

Pontiac, 11 miles (17km) west of Odell, took its name from a 17th century Ottawa Indian chief, whose face was used as a logo on signs for the Pontiac Trail – the pre-Route 66 highway between Chicago and St. Louis. Crossing the Vermillion River just outside the town, the highway continues southwest, with I-55 close by, passing through Lexington and Towanda, and on towards Normal and Bloomington, which share the same Main Street. Normal was the site of the first "Steak

'n Shake" restaurant, opened in 1934 by local entrepreneur Gus Belt – whose company lived up to its famous motto, "in sight it must be right," by preparing its hamburgers where diners could see them. The "Steak 'n Shake" chain went on to establish itself throughout Illinois and beyond; after Gus Belt's death in 1954, it was managed for many years by his widow, Edith.

About 10 miles (16km) beyond Bloomington, a roadside sign directs visitors to Funks Grove, a small community established by the Funk family in the 1820s. The grove is famous for its maple sirup,

| 0099 | | Chenoa | | 0118 | | Towanda | | 0137 | | Funks Grove | | 0152 | | Lincoln | | 0177 |
| Pontiac | | 0108 | | Lexington | | 0126 | | Normal/Bloomington | | 0147 | | McLean | | 0167 | | Broadwell |

FUNKS GROVE

Maple sirup is made at Funks Grove for just a few weeks in February and March each year. Approximately 6500 individual holes are drilled about three inches (7.6cm) into the trees (which must be at least 40 years old before they are ready to be tapped), and metal spouts – some attached to buckets, others connected to pipelines – are hammered in to collect the sap. When first extracted, it is watery in appearance and not especially sweet; both color and flavor are enhanced by the process of boiling and evaporation that turns the raw liquid into sirup. Its production is very rare in this region, and the maple trees themselves are a valuable natural resource, which have been preserved for many years by the Funk family, and their close relatives the Stubblefields, without any public subsidy.

Above: The family-run shop at Funks Grove sells maple sirup and souvenirs to a worldwide clientele.

which the Funks began to produce commercially in 1891. Today, the family business is run by Stephen Funk (great-grandson of the settlement's founder, Isaac), his wife Glaida, and their son and daughter-in-law. The Funks' maple plantation occupies about 1600 acres (650ha). Sap is gathered from the trees via taps and buckets, and boiled down before being bottled; approximately 50 gallons (190lit) are needed to produce a single gallon (c.4lit) of sirup. The delicious finished product is shipped to customers throughout America and Europe, and can also be purchased at the Grove itself.

From here, it is only a short distance to the next major town on the Old Road, McLean – a perennially popular place for travelers to break their journey, and the site of 66's first-ever truck stop, the Dixie Trucker's Home.

Dixie Trucker's Home

Below: Menu card for the café at McLean's famous Dixie Trucker's Home. A family business, it has missed only one day's trading since it opened in 1928, and is one of Route 66's best-known and most popular eateries.

J.P. Walters and his son-in-law, John Geske, opened McLean's Shirley Oil and Supply Company (named for a tiny settlement located southwest of Bloomington) in 1928. Route 66 had been in existence for less than two years, but Walters and Geske had already foreseen the needs of long-distance travelers. From the start, their roadside business, soon rechistened the Dixie Trucker's Home, offered food and coffee as well as diesel and gas; and in the 1930s, with the introduction of 24-hour service, the Dixie became 66's first recognized truckstop. The choice of its name – a curious one to use in the mid-West – was explained by John Geske in Susan Croce Kelly and Quinta Scott's book *Route 66*. "There was a time in this part of the country when people thought if they went south they would find more hospitality, so we thought Dixie was a good name. And it has proved to be that way. Dixie has had a friendly ring over the years."

J.P. Walters – a hands-on boss, who could often be seen working in the kitchens alongside his staff – remained in charge until his death in 1950, when John Geske took over; the Dixie is currently owned and run by Mark Beeler (John's grandson) and his wife Kathy. Recently, the family firm has expanded, opening Dixie Truckers Homes in four other Illinois locations, as well as a truckstop in Pennsylvania, but the McLean Dixie remains at the heart of their business. Remarkably, it has been closed for just one day (due to a fire in 1965) throughout its seven-decade history. In 1967, it moved into new premises on its original site: these incorporate a café offering classic American road food like broiled chicken, burgers and homemade pie, as well as a garage, a gift shop, and a permanent display of Route 66 memorabilia.

Above: The Dixie welcomes all travelers, but the many powerful rigs parked outside are proof that it still appeals to its original customers - the truckers.

Left and right: The Dixie, with its distinctive logo, is a landmark on 66. Its founder, J.P. Walters, who had no connection with the South, chose the "Dixie" name to convey an image of friendliness and hospitality.

Below: Drivers on Route 66 needed accurate maps; the ones shown here were published by America's National Automobile Club, an organization founded in 1924, just as motoring was becoming widely popular.

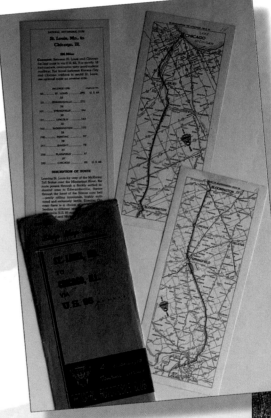

The area between McLean and Springfield has close associations with Abraham Lincoln (1809–1865), who lived in the Illinois state capital from 1837 until his election to the White House in 1861, making his reputation as a local lawyer and serving as a member of the House of Representatives between 1846 and 1849. In 1853, Postville, 15 miles (24km) beyond McLean, was renamed Lincoln in his honor; at a ceremony to mark the occasion, he is said to have used watermelon juice to "rechristen" the town!

Lincoln purchased a house on Springfield's Eighth and Jackson Streets in 1844, adding a second story to it 12 years later. The building and its surrounding neighborhood have been carefully preserved, and there are many other Lincoln-related sites in the city which he made his home. The President expressed his love for Springfield in the speech he gave before leaving for Washington in 1861: "No one, not in my situation, can appreciate my feeling of sadness at this parting. To this place, and the kindness of these people, I owe everything." He is buried in the city's Oak Ridge Cemetery.

The stretch of road around Springfield also includes several more recently built points of interest. Broadwell, a few miles southwest of Lincoln, was the location for one of 66's best-loved restaurants, the Pig Hip, which opened in 1937 and continued to serve customers until 1991; its proprietor, Ernie Edwards, still lives in a house nearby. Another Mecca for lovers of road food is Springfield's Cozy Drive In, founded in 1949 by Ed Waldmire, creator of the hugely popular "corn dog" – a deep-fried battered sausage on a stick. Since Ed's death in 1993, the Cozy has been run by his son, Buz, and distinctive, superbly detailed maps and drawings of Route 66 by another Waldmire brother, Bob, are also on sale and display there.

Right: The Lincoln House at 8th and Jackson in downtown Springfield – the future President's home for some 17 years. Visitors can walk around the neighborhood, and enjoy a special exhibition devoted to Lincoln's life in Springfield at the nearby Harriet Dean House.

• VOICE OF THE ROAD •

Bob Waldmire

Bob Waldmire's earliest attempt at map-making was a "bird's-eye" poster of his hometown, Springfield, produced during his student days. Subsequently, his love for the open road led him to adopt a nomadic existence, living in a camper van, and drawing the animals, plants, and scenery he encountered on his travels.

In an interview with Tom Teague of Route 66 *Magazine, Bob explained the special affinity with 66 that inspired his magnum opus – the "nostalgic, bioregionally-flavored" map of the highway he published in 1992. "I try and sensitize the viewer and reader to nature...[and] on 66 there was this...feeling of being closer to the land and nature."*
On a journey from Arizona to Illinois, as he told Teague, "the light bulb lit that I should make a map about Route 66. Initially, I thought I'd knock [it] out in a few months, [but] it ended up taking sixteen pages and four years."

Above: Two sausages get "Cozy" at the famous drive-in founded by Ed Waldmire on Springfield's South 6th Street. Ed ran the business until shortly before his death in 1991; it is now operated by his son Buz.

Right: The front of the Cozy Drive In, embellished by Bob Waldmire's vivid and distinctive signs and hand-drawn maps.

29

Right: "IDOT" stands for Illinois Department of Transportation – but this sign, by the side of Route 66 a few miles north of Litchfield, could easily be misread by inattentive passing motorists!

Below: "Our Lady of the Highways" - a shrine to the Virgin Mary on the Old Road near Waggoner. This marble statue, whose pedestal is sometimes decorated with bunches of flowers and other offerings from travelers, has stood here since the late 1950s.

The pre-1930 Springfield-Staunton section of Route 66 overlaps with IL4, heading through Chatham, Auburn (where there is a rare stretch of brick pavement), Virden and Carlinville. However, most modern travelers follow the Old Road's later, more direct alignment via Divernon, Farmersville, and Waggoner. This passes a remarkable roadside shrine: a Carrara marble statue of the Virgin Mary, which has stood on land belonging to farmer Francis Marten since 1959. Mr. Marten's daughter, Loretta, was a member of the group of local Catholic Youth Organizations from surrounding parishes that raised the $400 needed to import the statue from Italy; when it arrived, he and his family provided a site for it, and have continued to tend it ever since. The statue has become known as "Our Lady of the Highways," and the plaque beneath it carries a prayer for travelers: "Mary loving Mother of Jesus protect us on the highway."

Fifteen miles (24km) south of Waggoner lies Litchfield – described in 1946 by the author of the first-ever guide to Route 66, Jack D. Rittenhouse, as "an old mining town, and...the locale of early oil production." Mines and derricks are now long gone, but Litchfield remains a significant staging post on the Old Road, while nearby Lake Lou Yaeger (just to the northeast) offers excellent facilities for camping,

| 0228 | Waggoner | 0246 | Mt. Olive | 0260 | Hamel | 0279 | Mitchell | |
| Farmersville | 0232 | Litchfield | 0254 | Staunton | 0270 | Edwardsville | 0288 | *Mississippi River* |

> 66 **That the poorest and most thinly populated countries would be greatly benefited by the opening of good roads…is what no person will deny. But yet it is folly to undertake works of this or any other kind, without first knowing that we are able to finish them – as half finished work generally proves to be labor lost.** 99

from Abraham Lincoln's first political statement, addressed to the People of Sangamo County, Illinois, March 9, 1832

Above: Road signs like this make it easy to follow 66 through Illinois.

Below: Litchfield's Ariston Café dates from 1924.

Above: Litchfield's Route 66 Café, proudly displaying its classic "66" shield - the original marker for the Old Road, now adopted by many businesses operating alongside the highway.

boating, swimming, and other outdoor pursuits. The town boasts two impressive roadside restaurants: the Ariston Café and Route 66 Café. The Ariston, on South Old Route 66, has been run by the Adam family since it opened in 1924; its wide-ranging menu includes Western, Italian, and Mexican dishes. The Route 66, about half a mile further south (just beyond the railroad crossing), occupies the site of an old tourist court and is an elegant, art deco-influenced diner.

Excelsior Super-X

Excelsior's Super-X sold for $325, weighed about 450lb (204kg) and had a top speed of 65mph (105kph).

The Super-X shown here is a 1930 model owned by Otis Chandler of Ojai, California. In its six years of production, several changes were made to the model's basic design, including the enclosure of its exhaust valves and the addition of a front brake.

Chicago's Excelsior Supply Company was set up in 1876 to produce pedal cycles; its first engine-powered machine, the 3.25hp Excelsior Auto-Cycle, appeared in 1907. Three years later, the firm was acquired by the bicycle maker Ignatz Schwinn. Excelsior provided fierce competition to its larger rivals, Harley-Davidson and Indian, and its

750cc Super-X, launched in 1925, was successful on both road and racetrack; but the company could not survive the onset of the Depression, and closed in 1931. However, the marque has recently been revived by David and Dan Hanlon, whose Excelsior-Henderson Motorcycle Manufacturing Company now produces a modern version of the Super-X.

After the appearance of the Excelsior Super-X, Indian and Harley-Davidson quickly introduced their own 750cc models.

The machine has an IOE (inlet over exhaust) V-twin engine developing 20 horsepower.

Below: Old oil-cans and other garage artifacts are now becoming collectors' items; these examples were photographed at the National Route 66 Museum in Clinton, OK.

Excelsior produced modified versions of the Super-X for off-road events like hillclimbing competitions.

The Frisina Sky View, on the outskirts of Litchfield, is one of the few surviving drive-in cinemas on Route 66. It remains closed throughout the winter months, but continues to present movies during Spring and Summer. The theater has moved with the times, advertising its current schedules on the Internet, and carrying its soundtracks on FM radio. This allows patrons to enjoy high quality audio through their in-car sound systems instead of relying on the "lo-fi" portable loudspeakers traditionally used at drive-ins. Admission to the Sky View is currently $1 per person, with no charge for children under six.

Eight miles (13km) further south is a telling reminder of Illinois' turbulent industrial history: Mount Olive Union Miners' Cemetery, which contains an impressive, 80-ton granite memorial to Mary Harris Jones – better known as "Mother Jones" (1830–1930). Jones first championed the cause of child workers, and subsequently became an

Above: Soulsby Shell Station, Mount Olive – built by Henry Soulsby in 1926 and operated by his family until 1997. It is now owned by Mike Dragovich, who maintains it in association with the Soulsby Station Society.

Top, right and far right: *The Frisina Sky View Drive In provides movie entertainment for thousands of patrons, but no longer opens during the winter months.*

indomitable crusader for miners' rights. Even a period of imprisonment, served at the age of 83, did not dampen her fervor, and after a lifetime of campaigning, she was buried at Mount Olive alongside the victims of the 1898 Virden mine riot.

After passing the historic Soulsby Shell Station, which opened in 1926 and continued to serve customers on the Old Road until 1991, Route 66 leaves Mount Olive and joins SR 157 for the last few miles of its journey through Illinois, heading for the flat, low-lying area around the Mississippi. It continues through Hamel (famous for its Church of the Neon Cross, which is illuminated at night) and Edwardsville before reaching a junction with I-270. The Interstate leads quickly toward the river, crossing just to the north of the famous Chain of Rocks Bridge used by 66 from the mid-1930s until 1968. There are also alternative, more southerly routes into St. Louis via I-64 or I-255.

“ **I hope it will be my consolation when I pass away to feel I sleep under the clay with those brave boys.** ”

Mary Harris "Mother" Jones, speaking of her bond with the miners whose cause she supported

Above: Entrance to the Mount Olive Union Miners' Cemetery. It was opened in 1898, when coal mining was a key industry in this area of Illinois.

Left: The Mother Jones Memorial – a tribute to the "Miners' Angel," Mary Harris Jones. Its bronze plaques commemorate the victims of the 1898 uprising at Virden, just to the north.

Missouri

After passing through St. Louis, the biggest urban center on Route 66 between Chicago and Los Angeles, the Old Road follows the path of even older highways and trails as it crosses the undulating, richly forested Ozark Plateau. Beyond Springfield, the terrain levels out, and at the western edge of the state, 66 continues toward Kansas, briefly diverging from the Interstate (I-44), which heads straight for Oklahoma.

Above: The Chain of Rocks Bridge. It once carried Route 66 over the Mississippi, and is now open to pedestrians and cyclists. Main picture: Looking east downhill from Gray Summit, about 35 miles (56km) beyond St. Louis.

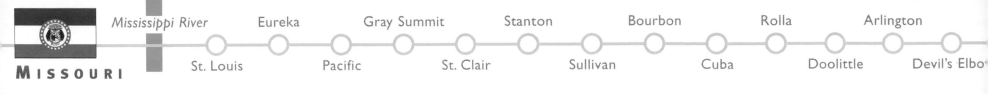
Missouri

Above: One of the many souvenir shields based on the classic Route 66 marker, combined here with a Missouri logo. Designs like this were never actually used as real road signs.

Before the advent of Route 66, the easiest way to cross Missouri was by railroad. The Pacific company began building its tracks southwest from St. Louis in the 1850s; and by 1883, the line, which had been taken over by the St. Louis and San Francisco Railway Company in 1876, extended through Pacific, Rolla, Arlington, Lebanon, and Springfield to Carthage and on into Kansas.

Highway transportation was less advanced, and as late as the World War I years, many of Missouri's major thoroughfares still had gravel or dirt surfaces. 1915 saw the formation of the Ozark Trails Association, which lobbied for the provision of adequate roads throughout the region; its prime movers included the "Father of Route 66," Cyrus Avery (see pages 10-13). Five years later, the state's voters approved a $60,000,000 bond issue to finance road building and "Get Missouri Out of the Mud." As Jim Powell explains in an article for *Route 66*

Magazine, almost 50 percent of this money was allocated to the improvement of Missouri's main highways, and "by the mid-1920s the construction program for pouring 'slab' (concrete) on the primary system…was well underway." Work progressed quickly: by 1927, 190 miles (306km) of the newly commissioned Route 66 in the state had been paved; and on St. Patrick's Day, 1931, celebrations were held in Rolla to mark the completion of concreting throughout its entire 310-mile (499km) length (see pages 44-45).

Right: 66 is often referred to as The Will Rogers Highway, in honor of the great Oklahoma-born entertainer.

Right: Vernelle's Motel on Sugar Tree Road, east of the infamous Devil's Elbow river crossing.

Below: The Diamonds Restaurant – now closed to customers, but once a popular attraction at Gray Summit.

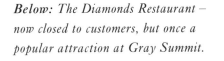

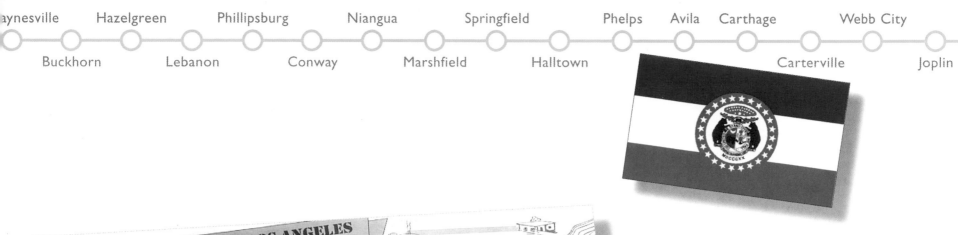

Today, nearly all of this can still be driven, although it is frequently necessary to cross the freeway to reach the various alignments. Few travelers will want to spend more time than is necessary on I-44, whose relentless pace seems utterly out of keeping with Missouri's predominately peaceful, rural surroundings. Unlike 44, Route 66 is an integral part of the landscape; its distinctive atmosphere often casts such a strong spell that it is possible to forget the existence of the Interstate, even when it lies only yards away. Here, as in so many other places, the Old Road has become, as Spencer Crump put it in his book *Route 66: America's First Main Street*, "both something in people's fantasies and a physical road on which a motorist can…enjoy scenery and people seemingly untouched by time."

Below: Looking east along 66's undulating south frontage near Arlington. The freeway is to the left.

Right: This drive-in, west of Carthage, was opened in 1949, and is still in regular use today.

39

Bridges

Below left: The 1916 road bridge across the Colorado, seen from the Topock, AZ side of the river ("Topock" is derived from the Mojave word for "bridge").
Below right: "Pony"-type bridge, in which parallel superstructures support the roadway, near Bridgeport, OK.

On its path from Chicago to Los Angeles, Route 66 traverses three mighty rivers – the Mississippi, Rio Grande, and Colorado – and a host of lesser ones. Building bridges across them sometimes presented formidable difficulties. Designers working on St. Louis' famous Chain of Rocks crossing in 1927 had to create a structure that would be adequate for cars and trucks while not obstructing the Mississippi's shipping. A number of experts believe this to be the reason for the bridge's curious 24-degree bend; the combination of straight and angled sections, though less than ideal for drivers, ensures the widest possible space between the piers for river traffic. The Chain of Rocks engineers faced other challenges, not least from the weather; ice and flooding caused extensive delays, and the bridge was a year behind schedule when it finally opened in 1929.

The Colorado River was an even more unfriendly location, and the builders of the first highway bridge across it at Topock doubtless learned from the mistakes of their nineteenth-century predecessors, whose railroad crossings had been repeatedly washed away during the 1880s. The Topock road bridge, a three-hinged arch design with a weight limit of 11 tons, was completed in February 1916, and used by Route 66 traffic until the end of World War II; it currently carries a natural gas pipeline over the Colorado.

Above: Parker Truss bridge at Rio Puerco, NM.
Right: Items relating to the Chain of Rocks Bridge (St. Louis, MO) on display at the headquarters of The Friends of Route 66 UK at the Drum Inn, Cockington, near Torquay, Devon.

Other, smaller scale Route 66 river bridges were made to standardized, "off-the-shelf" designs. Two types once widely employed throughout the USA were the Rainbow or Marsh Arch, named for its original developer, James Barney Marsh (1854–1936); and the Parker Truss, invented by Charles H. Parker. Both styles are now increasingly rare; the only surviving Rainbow Arch on 66 is the "Graffiti Bridge" near Baxter Springs, Kansas, while a carefully preserved Parker truss can be seen at the Rio Puerco, beyond Albuquerque.

| | St. Louis | 0324 | Pacific | 0334 | St. Clair | 0363 | Sullivan | 037 |
| Mississippi River | | 0299 | Eureka | 0331 | Gray Summit | 0349 | Stanton | 0369 | Bourb |

Above: The Coral Court Motel, a favorite overnight stop for travelers on 66, photographed before its demolition.

Below: Crestwood's "66" Park In Theatre dates from the late 1940s, and remained a popular attraction in this area for over four decades.

Although it is possible to follow I-270 around the perimeter of St. Louis, eventually turning onto I-44 to resume the journey west, it is well worth taking a detour to explore older alignments of 66 in the city and its suburbs. State 366 is one such route, heading along Chippewa Street (Ted Drewes Frozen Custard, makers of fine ice cream since 1930, can be found at No. 6726) to Watson Road. Here, in the Marlborough district, the Coral Court Motel once provided Route 66 users with comfortable, secluded overnight lodging; its Art Deco-style cabins were set in nearly nine acres of lawns and trees. The Coral Court opened in 1941, but went out of business in the 1990s; despite protests and petitions from road lovers and former guests, its buildings and grounds have now been destroyed.

Continuing west on Watson, 366 enters the suburb of Crestwood, and passes another relic from the Old Road's heyday, the now disused "66" Park In Theatre, whose huge screen still survives. The road then joins up with I-44, leading away toward the Sunset Hills district and across the Meramec River.

Once out of the city, the original path of Route 66 (usually running alongside the Interstate) is clearly signposted; alternatively, drivers can stay on I-44, exiting to visit places of interest that lie on or near the Old Road. One such site is the Black Madonna Shrine, a little way off Route 66, between the towns of Eureka and Pacific. It was created by Brother Bronislaus Luszcz, founder member of a community of Polish friars that settled in the area in 1927. Luszcz, who died in 1960, spent over 20 years working on the shrine; it comprises a chapel and seven grottoes, and is decorated with clamshells, jewelry, and other unusual objects provided by pilgrims.

Above: Ted Drewes Frozen Custard – a family business whose superb ice cream attracts customers from all over the USA.

CHAIN OF ROCKS BRIDGE

The Chain of Rocks Bridge (left and below), *named after the nearby rapids in the Mississippi, was completed in 1929. An impressive and expensive feat of engineering, spanning 5353 feet (1632m) and costing $2,000,000, its introduction shortened the journey time from Edwardsville, on the Illinois side of the river, by 15 miles (24km). However, the bridge's narrow roadway and the 24 degree bend at its midpoint made it potentially hazardous for drivers; in 1968, after the inauguration of I-270, it was closed to traffic and allowed to fall into disrepair. Recently, though, its fortunes have improved, thanks to Gateway Trailnet, a non-profitmaking organization that has successfully raised funds to restore the Chain of Rocks, open it to pedestrians and bicycles, and link it to a network of walking and cycling trails in both Missouri and Illinois.*

Mississippi River | 0299 | St. Louis | 0324 | Pacific | 0334 | St. Clair | 0363 | Sullivan | 0371
Eureka | 0331 | Gray Summit | 0349 | Stanton | 0369 | Bourb...

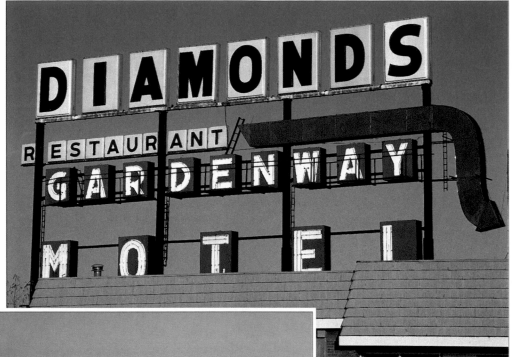

As 66 heads deeper into Missouri and toward the Ozark Plateau, the terrain gradually becomes more undulating and wooded. This is a land of mines (like those around the town of Pacific, which supply silica used to make glass and ceramics) and caves – most notably the Meramec Caverns near Stanton, first opened to the public in 1933, and advertised extensively along the Old Road as "the greatest show under the earth."

After leaving Pacific, we reach Gray Summit, and pass the gateway to the 1600-acre Shaw Arboretum, founded in 1926 as an outpost of the Missouri Botanical Garden in St. Louis. Nearby stands the Diamonds Restaurant, with another Route 66 landmark, the Gardenway Motel, adjacent to it. The Diamonds, known for decades as "the Old Reliable Eating Place," was relocated here in the 1960s, but has now closed; it previously occupied a site at Villa Ridge, a few miles to the west.

Above: Looking west from 66's south frontage beyond Doolittle. The north frontage road lies to the right, beyond the Interstate carriageways.

Right and above top: The Diamonds Restaurant and Gardenway Motel are both closed, but the adjacent parking lot remains a popular rest stop for truckers.

Route 66 continues via St. Clair and Stanton to Sullivan, birthplace of George Hearst (1820–1891), newspaper magnate William Randolph Hearst's father. The town's attractions include its beautiful Shamrock Motel, built from handcut Ozark stone. Many other settlements on this section of the road owe their origins to European émigrés who arrived in the region during the 19th century, and established the vineyards that still thrive around Bourbon and Cuba.

23 miles (37km) west of Cuba lies Rolla, once a station on the old "Wire Road," a military telegraph line constructed between Missouri and Arkansas in the 1850s and 1860s; Route 66 follows its route through much of the state. Rolla is steeped in highway history; in 1931, it was the focus of celebrations to mark the completion of paving on 66's Missouri section. Guests included Cyrus Avery, the Oklahoma businessman known as the "Father of the Mother Road."

Below: The wooded slopes surrounding the highway west of Doolittle contribute to the timeless, restful atmosphere on this section of the Old Road.

Below: Yet another adaption of the Route 66 shield – used by the Phillips Petroleum company to promote its best-selling brand of gasoline.

Right: An elegant old bridge carries Route 66 across the river west of Rolla. The Mark Twain National Forest surrounds the road for many miles in this part of Missouri.

45

Below: The road leading toward the bend in the Big Piney River known as Devil's Elbow was an accident black spot, although substantial improvements were made to it during the 1940s. In 1981, it became one of the last sections of Route 66 to be bypassed by I-44. This commemorative postcard shows an artist's impression of the cutoff, with a stylized Chevrolet Corvette approaching it.

Above: On the riverbank at Devil's Elbow – this is the narrow truss bridge that once carried all Route 66's traffic.

The route between Doolittle, about eight miles (13km) from Rolla, and Arlington, seven miles (11km) further on, is enjoyable but can be confusing. Both the northern and southern frontages alongside I-44 are worth exploring, but there are places where 66 seems to disappear or lead nowhere, and it is sometimes necessary to travel on the freeway. Arlington has been affected by changing highway alignments since World War II years, when its main street was cut off by a new stretch of road built around 1942. Perhaps this has contributed to the atmosphere of picturesque decline still apparent on the north frontage near the village. In the undergrowth by the roadside are the gradually decaying remains of "John's Modern Cabins" and Vernelle's Motel – described memorably by Jerry McClanahan in *Route 66 Magazine* as ruins where "once cash registers rang to the peal of commerce, [but] now only echoes of dim memories sigh through vacant window frames."

Above: This gateway, east of Devil's Elbow, commemorates the Native American "Trail of Tears" which passed nearby.

Another stretch of Old Road that seems to belong to a different era is the often deserted two-lane section of highway around Devil's Elbow, about four miles (6km) west of Arlington (beyond Interstate exit 172). Referred to in Jack D. Rittenhouse's *Guide Book to Highway 66* as "an odd geological formation," this sharp bend in the Big Piney River near Hooker may have acquired its name from lumberjacks whose logs became stuck there. It is a peaceful, tree-shaded place; however, before it was bypassed in the mid-1940s, it was notorious as a black spot for accidents, and it is easy to imagine the dangers posed to drivers by its winding pavements and narrow truss bridge. West of this hazardous section of Route 66 lie Waynesville (and the U.S. Army's massive training facility at nearby Fort Leonard Wood), Hazelgreen, and Lebanon.

| 0458 | Lebanon | | 0487 | Conway | 0497 | | Marshfield | 0529 | | Halltown | 0561 |
| Hazelgreen | | 0475 | Phillipsburg | 0492 | | Niangua | 0503 | Springfield | | 0549 | Phelps |

> " O highway I travel, do you say to me
> Do not leave me?
> Do you say Venture not – if you leave me you are lost?
> Do you say I am already prepared,
> I am well-beaten and undenied, adhere to me?
> O public road, I say back I am not afraid to leave you,
> yet I love you,
> You express me better than I can express myself,
> You shall be more to me than my poem. "

from Song of the Open Road *by Walt Whitman (1819–1892)*

Above: A deserted, peaceful stretch of 66 near Arlington; although I-44 lies quite close by, the steep embankment preserves the tranquility of the Old Road in this area.

Above and right: The picturesque ruins of "John's Modern Cabins" on Route 66's north frontage at Sugar Tree Road, just east of the Trail of Tears gateway.

Munger Moss Motel

Below: This vintage postcard shows the early layout of Lebanon's Munger Moss Motel; its individual cabins were subsequently replaced by the modern building shown in the main photograph.

The Munger Moss, a famous and still thriving Route 66 business, has existed, in different forms, at two sites on the Old Road in Missouri. For many years, it has been a motel on Lebanon's East Seminole Street, but it started out as a barbeque restaurant near Devil's Elbow, 48 miles (77km) east of town. Its first proprietors, Pete and Jessie Hudson, were obliged to relocate in 1945, after Route 66 was widened and diverted away from the dangerous stretch of road near their old premises. They moved to a café in Lebanon, the Chicken Shanty, bought some adjacent land, and set about building a "motor court" in the typical style of the period. At first, guests were housed in a series

Munger Moss Motel "on old Rt. 66" Lebanon, Missouri.- Built in 1946

of freestanding cabins incorporating garages; gradually more of these units were added, and the spaces between them were "joined up" with other rooms to create a modern motel layout.

In *Route 66* by Susan Croce Kelly and Quinta Scott, Jessie Hudson reminisces about her guests at the Munger Moss. These included showbiz stars who came to entertain army personnel at nearby Fort Leonard Wood — notably the Harry James Orchestra, who, as Mrs. Hudson recalls, "were always surrounded by autograph hounds. One morning…a lady there…was determined she would make the bed that Harry James had slept in. Just for meanness I told her another room, and later, when I told her right, Laws!

Right: The parking lot alongside the Munger Moss on Lebanon's East Seminole Street.

Above: The Munger Moss today – still thriving after more than more than half a century of service to travelers on Route 66.

I thought she would whip me!" In the Munger Moss's heyday, when 66 was the main artery for east-west traffic, there was rarely a dull moment for Jessie. "We had movie dogs; we had a giraffe stay all night...on his way to the Oklahoma City Zoo; we had helicopters land in the yard...There's never been a time in all these years I ever wished I was anyplace else."

Right: The historic Landers Theater on Springfield's Walnut Street. Kathleen Turner, who was born in the city, is one of several stars who made their early reputations on its stage.

Below: Looking east along a quiet stretch of Route 66 near Niangua, on the way to Springfield.

Above: Ads for the Meramec Caverns are a constant feature of 66 in Missouri. These two barns can be seen alongside the road east of Phillipsburg.

For much of the 54-mile (87km) journey from Lebanon to Springfield, the "Queen City of the Ozarks," the highway runs close to the old St. Louis and San Francisco ("Frisco") railroad line, which came to the area in the 1860s. Conway, about 17 miles (27km) southwest of Lebanon, is named after the contractor who built the section of track that runs through the town. Beyond Conway lies Marshfield (described in 1946 by Jack D. Rittenhouse as "a quiet, agricultural community, little touched by the rush of traffic"), and soon afterwards 66 approaches the suburbs of Springfield.

The city has seen its share of unrest and conflict. Just to the south is the site of one of the bloodiest encounters of the Civil War, The Battle of Wilson's Creek, which took place on August 10,1861; many of the soldiers who died there are buried in the National Cemetery at Glenstone and Seminole.

Springfield is also famous for its links with J.B. "Wild Bill" Hickok (1837–1876). On Central Square, a pair of small plaques set into the road commemorate Wild Bill's shoot-out (provoked by a gambling dispute) with Confederate drifter Dave Tutt on July 21, 1865. The plaques mark the two men's relative positions during the gunfight, in which Tutt was killed by Hickok; visitors need to be careful of oncoming traffic while locating and examining them! Wild Bill was subsequently cleared

of Tutt's murder, but the incident seems to have confirmed his reputation as a "desperado" and "a drunken swaggering fellow." Unsurprisingly, the local citizens rejected him when he ran for marshal a few years later.

Springfield's many other attractions include the historic Landers Theater on Walnut Street, dating from 1909; and the extraordinary red brick and terracotta Shrine Mosque at St. Louis and Kimbrough, built in 1923 and recently refurbished.

Below: There was little love lost between Wild Bill Hickok and Dave Tutt, who resorted to a gun duel after falling out over a card game in July 1865. Tutt died at this spot in Springfield's Central Square before he had time to draw his weapon.

> **No quiet-turned man could or would care to take the office of marshal, which jeopardized his life; hence the necessity of employing a desperado – one who feared nothing and would as soon shoot an offending subject as look at him.**

Joseph G. McCoy writing of "Wild Bill" Hickok in **Historic Sketches of the Cattle Trade of the West and Southwest,** *1874*

Above: One of the plaques in Central Square, Springfield, marking the positions of Hickok and Tutt during their 1865 shootout
Left: A typically undulating section of 66 as it heads through the Ozark region.

Below: Bernie's Route 66 Bar, east of Avila – a welcome sight for travelers who may have been unnerved by the "hellfire" signs (see right) that appear just up the road!

West of Springfield, we follow SR266 to just beyond Halltown. Here, SR96 continues toward Carthage, with surviving sections of 66's original alignment running nearby. The land in this area is lower and more level than the Ozark scenery further east. However, there is still plenty to see and to surprise – including, a few miles outside Avila, a series of "hellfire" roadside signs, in the style of the old Burma Shave ads, reminding us that we are in the Bible Belt!

Above: A vintage postcard displays the ultimate in luxurious accommodation at a Joplin hotel court.

Carthage, like Springfield, has strong Civil War associations. After the Union forces were defeated here by the Missouri State Guard in 1861, the area was targeted by Southern fighters, including the young Myra Maybelle Shirley – later to become notorious as Belle Starr. The city's Civil War Museum, on East Grant Street, provides a wealth of information about the Battle of Carthage and its aftermath, and includes an impressive 7 x 15-feet (2 x 4.5m) mural by local artist Andy Thomas.

Almost 7.5 miles (12km) of the road between Carthage and Joplin had been paved as early as 1920, according to historian Susan Croce Kelly. This stretch of highway, which subsequently became a part of Route 66, was designed to carry heavy traffic to and from the mines around Carterville and Webb City. It is worth taking a detour off US71 (now the main Carthage-Joplin route) to see the two old towns, as well as Jack Dawson's striking "Praying Hands" sculpture, with its inscription "Hands in Prayer – World in Peace," erected at Webb City in 1973.

BUT YOU SCRATCH IT JUST THE SAME

THEY USED TO CALL IT SIN...

NOW THEY CALL IT NEW MORALITY

BUT YOU GO TO HELL JUST THE SAME

Above: These alarming signs are visible to westbound traffic on 66 heading toward Avila. Eastbound travelers on this stretch of road are shown a succession of biblical texts.

Above: This rusting jalopy has been transformed into a striking road sign – it was photographed beside Route 66 east of Carthage.

At Joplin, 71 connects with SR66, which leads west to the state line. About five miles (8km) from this junction, take the turning marked "Old Route 66 next right." This alignment of the highway leads across the border and toward the town of Galena – our first destination in Kansas.

· VOICE OF THE ROAD ·

Frank Campbell

ROUTE 66 gave a massive boost to the trucking industry, and one of the first entrepreneurs to take advantage of its possibilities was Frank Campbell, who set up his Campbell "66" Express Company in Springfield, Missouri in 1933. Frank had run local haulage businesses since the 1920s, and already had a distinctive logo for his trucks: a camel, standing beside palm trees and a pyramid. However, after the threat of a lawsuit from the makers of Camel cigarettes, this image was modified by painter Bill Boyd, who gave the previously "stationary" camel galloping legs and steaming nostrils, added a "66" to its hump, and was responsible for renaming it "Snortin' Norton." The distinctive "66" Express fleet (with its memorable corporate slogan, "Humpin' to Please") eventually expanded to provide cargo transportation in over twenty states; but the decommissioning of the Old Road and the deregulation of the trucking industry proved fatal to the company, which closed in 1986.

Dodge Charger

ROUTE 66

*Above: Striped for action –
the Charger's distinctive
badge and sidetrim.*

The 1968 Dodge Charger is not a car for the faint-hearted. It was branded the "beautiful screamer" by the company's publicity, which went on to describe it as "American guts with more than a touch of Old World class – with something very un-Old World-like under its bonnet." That something was the Magnum V8 engine, producing 375bhp (425 on the extra-powerful Hemi model) and capable of propelling the Charger from 0-60mph (0-96kph) in under 7 seconds. Aggression is built into every aspect of this vehicle: it was conceived by Chrysler (Dodge's parent company) as a weapon in its "horsepower wars" with General Motors and Ford, and its reputation as a "muscle car" was sealed after its appearance in the 1968 movie *Bullitt*, starring Steve McQueen. The Charger went on to feature in many other 1960s and 1970s films and TV shows – and recently, animator Matt Groening used a cartoon version of it to chase Bart and run over Chief Wiggum in *The Simpsons*!

The Dodge Charger's appearance was inspired by Bill Brownlie, the company's head of design, who wanted the car to look "extremely masculine...like it had been lifted off the Daytona track."

The Charger's steel body and sleek profile were complemented by an all-black interior with foam-padded vinyl seating. A clock, illuminated ashtray, and cigarette lighter were fitted as standard.

Dodge boasted that the Charger's suspension "knows its way through the esses – as if the car were on rails."

Left: The V8 engines fitted to Chargers were very heavy – the Hemi model shown here weighed in at 765lb (347kg) – but exceptionally powerful.

Above: Pull up to the bumper – but beware of the blast from the Charger's twin exhausts!

Kansas

The 13-mile (21km) path taken by 66 through Kansas includes just three towns (Galena, Riverton, and Baxter Springs). It is, nevertheless, a significant segment of the Old Road, with links to the state's fascinating, sometimes turbulent history. As Tom Snyder comments in his *Route 66 Traveler's Guide*, "This place is a big part of the true America we all carry somewhere in our hearts."

Above: A roadside sign bearing the emblem of the "Sunflower State" greets Route 66 travelers on the Kansas/Oklahoma border.
Main picture: An aerial view of part of southeastern Kansas, through which the Old Road passes.

Kansas

Below: No one knows who first described 66 as the "Main Street of America:" the slogan appears on several early maps and was soon in wide use. However, the "straight-line" illustration of the highway on this vintage flyer is quite a piece of artistic licence!

The southeastern corner of Kansas lies near the end of the Shawnee Trail, once a major route for the movement of cattle. The Shawnee led from Texas, via Fort Gibson, Oklahoma, to various destinations in Kansas and Missouri; by the late 1860s, Baxter Springs (which had been settled barely a decade before) had become one of the busiest of these. According to William G. Cutler's *History of the State of Kansas*, published in 1883, it was a wild, unruly place, where "society was in a state of chaos...Bawdy and dance houses of the most virulent character were numerous, and the town, especially during the season when the cattle were being driven in, was in one continuous state of uproar, night and day."

Baxter Springs' prosperity was severely damaged when the cattle trail was moved northwest to Abilene shortly afterwards, as the result of legislation to prevent the infection of local livestock with the virulent "Texas fever" transmitted by ticks on the incoming longhorns. However, at about the same time, substantial mineral deposits were discovered a few miles to the northeast, leading to the establishment of another boom town, Galena, in the 1870s.

William G. Cutler paints an unflattering picture of early Galena: "The city [is] made up mostly of cheap and rough board shanties. The ground upon which it stands...is rendered unsightly by the heaps of excavated material...thrown from the mining and prospecting shafts in every part of it." But its need for supplies and transportation quickly led to the establishment of a railroad station (on the Kansas City, Fort Scott & Gulf line that already served Baxter Springs), and the provision of suitable highways followed soon afterwards.

Ads like these were once an everyday part of Route 66's landscape, displayed on the walls and windows of thousands of roadside stores and diners. Many are now collectors' items.

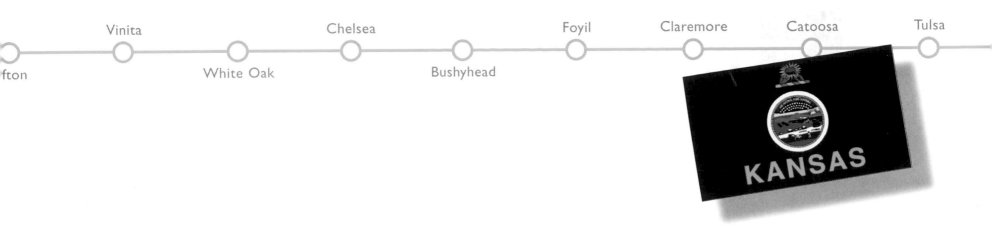

The mines were still thriving in the 1920s, and it was logical for Cyrus Avery's committee to route their new road through this key industrial area – although it lies north of the most direct path from Missouri to Oklahoma. Kansas proved to be second only to Illinois in the speed with which it paved its stretch of 66; concreting started soon after the commissioning of the highway, and was completed by 1929.

Today, driving the Old Road through the state is easy, thanks to the distinctive "sunflower" route markers; and the absence of the Interstate (which bypassed the area in the early 1960s) makes the journey all the more enjoyable.

Left: This superbly preserved old U.S. Army tank can be seen near Galena's Howard Litch Museum.

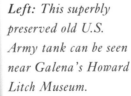

59

Joplin
Missouri

KANSAS

Galena
0615 Riverton

0618

Baxter Springs
0625

Oklahoma

Quapaw

Commerce

Miami

Below: The Kansas version of the "Historic Route 66" marker provides a helpful guide for drivers on the Old Road through the state – and is also painted onto the highway itself in some places (see right for an example).

Galena lies just two miles (3km) across the border from Missouri. Its original 120-acre (50ha) site was purchased from a German farmer by the Galena Mining & Smelting Company in 1877; historian William G. Cutler observed that "the excitement caused [by the discovery of lead and zinc in the area] was so great, that no sooner was a lot staked off than a purchaser was ready with the money in hand to buy it." During the boom years at the end of the 19th century, the town was a wild, rowdy place, with a main drag – nicknamed "Red Hot Street" – crowded with bars and bordellos. Prohibition and a stern moral climate (Tom Snyder, in his *Route 66 Traveler's Guide*, describes the area as "pretty close to the buckle on the Bible Belt") subsequently put paid to these excesses. However, Galena remained a troubled, sometimes violent

community throughout the 1920s and 1930s, when attacks on strike breakers and inter-union feuds led to a number of riots and shootings.

By the 1940s, many of the larger mines were exhausted. Jack D. Rittenhouse, writing about Galena in 1946, commented that "[the town's] growth seems to have slowed," although a few smaller workings still continued, and mounds of waste material from them (known as "chert" or "chat") remained a persistent eyesore. Today, even these have disappeared, but Galena's industrial heritage can be studied in its Mining and Historical Museum, housed in a former Missouri-

Above: Evening falls on Galena's Main Street. Today, the peaceful little town displays little trace of its wild past; this area was once a byword for drunkenness, violence, and debauchery.

Above and left: Galena's Howard Litch Museum Building, with an old Burlington Northern loco (of the type used on the Missouri-Kansas-Texas railroad through the town) on display outside.

Kansas-Texas railroad depot on Main Street. This was set up in 1983 by Howard T. Litch (1906–1990), a local resident who devoted much of his life to preserving his community's past.

A few miles outside Galena, the road crosses the Spring River (the 1920s Marsh Rainbow Arch bridge originally used by 66 was demolished in 1986) and enters Riverton.

Right: Looking across to Route 66 from one of the two local burial grounds that lie close to the Old Road on the outskirts of Galena.

Joplin
Missouri

KANSAS

Galena

0615

0618

Riverton

Baxter Springs

0625

Oklahoma

Quapaw

Commerce

Miami

Below: _Baxter Springs owed its early prosperity to cattle and cowboys; this mural by John Gibbins, reflecting the city's past, can be seen near the intersection of its Military and 11th Avenues._

Below right: _Café on the Route, just across the street from the Gibbins mural, occupies the site of a building alleged (like several others in this area) to have been raided by Jesse James._

After crossing the bridge, follow US 66 into Riverton. An essential port of call here is the Eisler Brothers General Store, run by Scott Nelson, President of the Kansas Historic Route 66 Association. With its "Main Street of America" sign, and the "66" shield painted onto the pavement outside, this well-known landmark is almost impossible to miss; in June 2000, it celebrated 75 years of service to local customers and travelers.

Beyond Riverton, continue west on the Old Road. Just over three miles (5km) from here, 66 approaches a Rainbow Arch-style bridge spanning

Left: A Mecca for devotees of the Old Road – Riverton's Eisler Brothers General Store is used by its owner, Scott Nelson, as the headquarters for Kansas' Historic Route 66 Association.

Below right: Bill Murphey's Route 66 Café, Baxter Springs. The road sign for Alt-69 (as 66 is named here) can be seen on the lamp post outside.

Brush Creek, similar in construction to the one that formerly crossed the Spring River (see pages 60–61). The Brush Creek bridge, dating from 1923, is covered by inscriptions that have earned it the nickname "Graffiti Bridge;" it was listed on the National Registry of Historic Places in 1983, and has recently been restored.

About four miles (6km) down the road is Baxter Springs – the final town on the short Kansas stretch of 66. In 1863, only five years after its foundation, it became the location for one of the bloodiest massacres of the Civil War, when Confederate forces led by Lt. Col. William C. Quantrill captured 87 Union soldiers and shot them in the back of the head. A memorial to the murdered men can be seen in the cemetery to the west of town.

For many years, Baxter Springs was an important staging post for cattle drovers, and the murals on its 11th Avenue are a reminder of its status as "the first cow town in Kansas." It also attracted the attention of Jesse James, who allegedly attacked a downtown bank on the site of what is now Bill Murphey's Route 66 Café in 1876. The old bank building and its history are featured in detail on the next two pages.

Top: The so-called "Graffiti" Rainbow Arch bridge that carries Route 66 over Brush Creek, a few miles outside Baxter Springs. Bridges of this type are sometimes also known as "Marsh Arches," after their creator, James Barney Marsh (1854–1936).

Murphey's Route 66 Café

Bill Murphey's Route 66 Café opened in 1941, but its site on Baxter Springs' Military Avenue has been occupied since 1868, when John M. Cooper, a migrant from Illinois, started a grocery and dry goods business there. In 1886, Cooper moved his shop (known as the Illinois Cash Store) one block south; and 14 years later he built new premises on the original site to house the Baxter Bank, with a Masonic Lodge hall upstairs.

The fact that there was no bank here until the 1900s seems to give the lie to the story about Jesse James' raid in 1876 (see preceding pages); James was not known for holding up grocery stores! However, there is no doubt that the Baxter National Bank (as it subsequently became) was attacked in 1914 by Henry Starr, "The Cherokee Badman" (1873–1921), who pulled off a series of audacious raids in Kansas and Oklahoma between 1913 and 1915. Starr, one quarter Indian, and a distant relative of "outlaw queen" Belle Starr (see pages 52-53), may have netted up to $60,000 from his 28-year criminal career, which ended after he was fatally wounded during a shoot-out in Arkansas. On his death bed, he boasted to doctors that he had "robbed more banks than any man in America."

The Baxter National Bank eventually moved away from this site (it merged with the American National Bank in 1952), but many of its features have been lovingly preserved in Bill Murphey's café. Vintage checks can be seen on the tabletops, the walls are covered with photos and plaques providing details of the building's history, and Mary Wilson, granddaughter of the Bank's former manager, is a regular customer here. Even the original bank vault is still in use – it has been converted into a ladies' rest-room!

Above and right: Old checks like these are preserved beneath the glass surface of the tables at Bill Murphey's Café – formerly the Baxter National Bank.

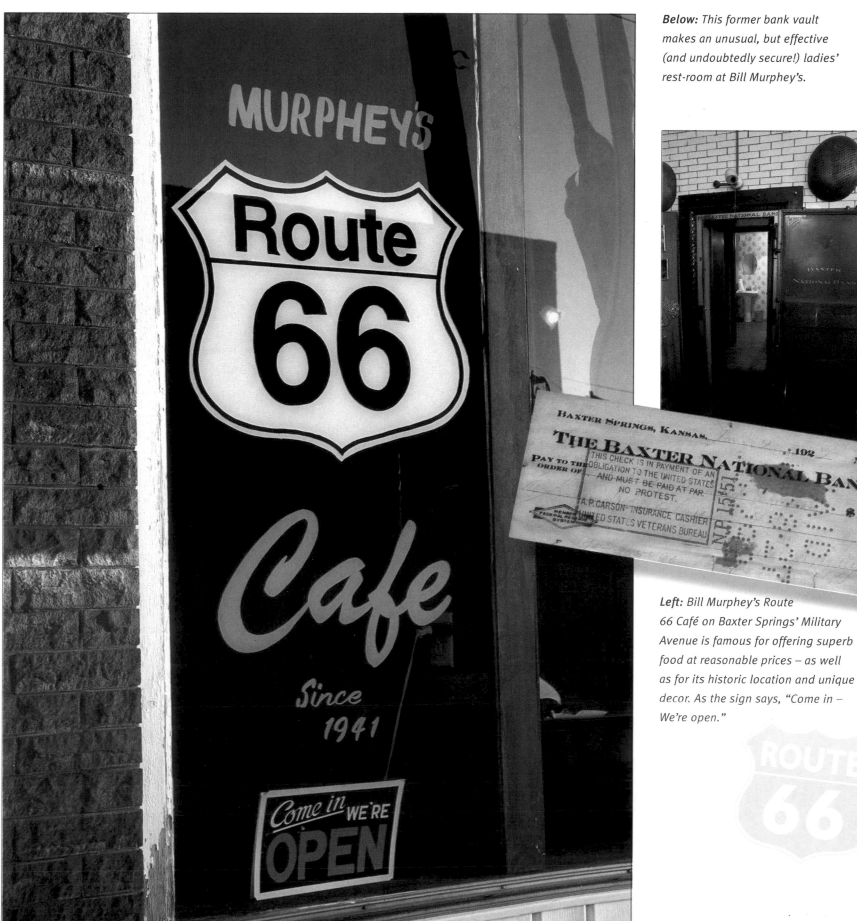

Below: *This former bank vault makes an unusual, but effective (and undoubtedly secure!) ladies' rest-room at Bill Murphey's.*

MURPHEY'S

Route 66

Cafe

Since 1941

Come in WE'RE OPEN

BAXTER SPRINGS, KANSAS,
THE BAXTER NATIONAL BANK
PAY TO THE ORDER OF

Left: *Bill Murphey's Route 66 Café on Baxter Springs' Military Avenue is famous for offering superb food at reasonable prices – as well as for its historic location and unique decor. As the sign says, "Come in – We're open."*

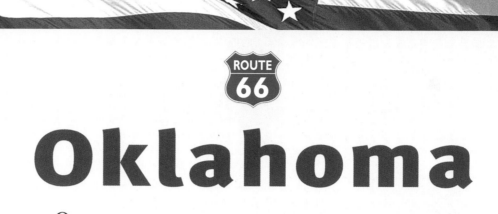

Oklahoma

Oklahoma has a special place in the history of Route 66. The prime mover in the highway's creation, Tulsa resident Cyrus Avery, lobbied tirelessly for it to pass through this region; and both 66 and part of I-44 were later named for another famous local figure, entertainer Will Rogers. The road stretches from the "Green Country" on the Sooner State's eastern borders to its western prairie lands.

Above: Lucille's service station, just southwest of Hydro - owned and operated by Lucille Hamons, the "Mother of the Mother Road," from 1941 until her death in 2000.
Main picture: Travelers are unlikely to overlook the huge sign advertising this tiny motel in downtown Yukon!

Oklahoma

Below: Unusually, this handbill promoting the pleasures of the Old Road incorporates the symbols of the five major Interstate highways that have replaced it as the "shortest and fastest" route to the Western states.

"As bad as the roads were in the rest of the United States," writes Susan Croce Kelly in her study of *Route 66: The Highway and its People*, "they were probably worse in Oklahoma, simply because [it] had remained unsettled and undeveloped longer than anywhere else." In the years immediately after it achieved statehood in 1907, this lack of proper highways was a major obstacle to the region's development – and no one strove more effectively to remedy the problem than Tulsa-based businessman Cyrus Avery, who became a Commissioner for the district where he lived in 1912. The post gave Avery special responsibility for roads, and he used his powers to lobby for local control over their construction.

By the 1920s, as a Highway Commissioner for Oklahoma and a key figure in the American Association of State Highway Officials, Avery was able to influence broader road-building policy. During discussions over the direction for what was to become Route 66, he insisted that it should run through his home state – even though this meant deviating from the path of established trails, most of which, in Susan Croce Kelly's words, "had gone around the place that later became Oklahoma." After winning this battle (in the face of fierce opposition from some of his colleagues) Avery was energetic in his efforts to get the new highway adequately surfaced. By 1937, its entire 370-mile (596km) length from Quapaw to Texola had been paved; and thanks to careful preservation and good signposting, nearly all of this is still accessible today.

Cyrus Avery planned a road; but in just a few years, Route 66 in Oklahoma took on a significance that he could not have foreseen, as the highway came to represent the dream of escape to a better life for

Below: Route 66 made Oklahoma an important center for transportation; road haulage businesses like the one advertised here were vital to its prosperity.

Below right: As we head west, Native American artifacts and artwork become increasingly common roadside sights.

the Okies stricken by the dust storms of the 1930s. The spirit of their struggles and restless travels was first captured in the songs of Woody Guthrie (1912–1967), a native Oklahoman who had hit the road himself at the age of 16. And in 1939, Route 66 became "the Mother Road" when John Steinbeck (1902–1968) published *The Grapes of Wrath*; his novel's haunting descriptions of the highway and its landscape retain a powerful resonance for anyone making the same journey today.

> *Right: An abandoned section of road near Hext, with a faded but still forbidding warning sign.*
> *Lower right: Okie singer-songwriter Woody Guthrie's autobiography,* Bound For Glory, *was filmed in 1976; this poster for the movie, quoting a line from Guthrie's famous song, "This Land Is Your Land," is signed by its star, David Carradine.*

Below: A model of the sign for the Will Rogers Motor Court in Tulsa. Sadly, the real building was destroyed some years ago.

Above: An effective anti-littering sign by the roadside at Vinita.

Below left: The biggest McDonald's in the world straddles the Will Rogers Turnpike (I-44) near Vinita.

Route 66 enters Oklahoma on Highway 69A; as a nearby sign suggests, native Americans once occupied this region, and the town of Quapaw, about five miles (8km) from the border, is named for the tribe who lived there until the 1830s. The Old Road continues through Commerce – childhood home of Micky Mantle (1931–1995), star baseball player for the New York Yankees, and holder of the record for the longest homerun ever measured in the history of his sport – and on toward Miami. Just to the east is I-44 (known here as the Will Rogers Turnpike), which runs direct from Missouri, bypassing Kansas, and now stays fairly close to 66 all the way to Oklahoma City.

However, travelers on the Turnpike see only the edges of Miami and other towns on the route west. Route 66 takes us down their Main Streets, allowing us to absorb their atmosphere and enjoy their distinctive architecture. Miami's most memorable building is its spectacular, Spanish Mission Revival-style Coleman Theater at 103 North Main, which opened in April 1929. Commissioned by a local businessman, George L. Coleman Sr., and designed by the Boller Brothers of Kansas City, who also created Albuquerque's KiMo Theater (see pages 126-127), it is now owned by the City of Miami, and continues to attract substantial audiences while raising funds for an ongoing restoration program.

About 10 miles (16km) south of the town, the highway crosses beneath I-44, and we follow US 60 for the journey to Afton. The town, established in 1886, was named for a river in Ayrshire, Scotland, by an Edinburgh-born railroad supervisor who was working nearby. Beyond it, 60 heads southwest toward another intersection with I-44 near Vinita. At this point, it is worth joining the Turnpike to see the world's largest McDonald's, which lies nearby; known as the Glass House before its takeover by the hamburger chain, it was the first restaurant ever constructed across a public highway in America.

Right: Abandoned quarry workings adjacent to the Old Road about 4 miles (6km) east of Quapaw.

0702
Catoosa
0731
Sapulpa
0750
Bristow
0800
Luther
0828

Claremore
0714
Tulsa
0741
Kellyville
0768
Chandler
0819
Arcadia

**ENTERING
INDIAN TERRITORY**

IN 1833, THIS AREA CEDED QUAPAW
TRIBE BY U.S. LANDS NEAR GRANTED
INDIANS OF 20 TRIBES INCLUDING
SENECA, SHAWNEE, PEORIA, MIAMI,
OTTAWA, WYANDOT. WEALTH CAME TO
THE QUAPAW AND TO OTHER INDIANS
HERE, FROM DISCOVERY OF RICH LEAD
AND ZINC MINES BEGINNING 1905.

OKLAHOMA HISTORICAL SOCIETY
164-1995

*Above: This marker, near the Oklahoma
state line, recalls the region's Indian heritage.
Right: The Thunderbird Motel which is
situated on Miami's Main Street.
Below: Miami's historic Coleman Theater.*

Thunderbird
MOTEL

VACANCY

WELCOME
NICE ROOMS
FREE HBO

Above: Claremore's Will Rogers Hotel, as modeled by The Cat's Meow Village - an item from the company's "theme collection" of 66-related miniatures.

Vinita, originally called Downingville, took its current name from a local sculptress, Vinita Ream, creator of the statue of Abraham Lincoln at the US Capitol in Washington. The town also has strong connections with Will Rogers, who attended school here, and whose annual Memorial Rodeo is still held nearby. Beyond Vinita, we join SR 66 where it meets US 60, and continue down the Old Road (now running north of the Turnpike) towards White Oak, about two miles (3km) away.

Further west lie Chelsea (with its replica of Oklahoma's first oil well) and Bushyhead; 66 then reaches Foyil, birthplace of Andy Payne (1907–1977), the runner who won the 3400-mile (5475km) L.A. to New York road race known as the "Bunion Derby," held in 1928.

Above and top: In its heyday, the Will Rogers Hotel (opened in 1930) provided the last word in elegant and luxurious accommodation; its many attractions included spa water baths fed from Claremore's nearby artesian spring.

Above: A fitting tribute to a distinguished athlete: a memorial in downtown Foyil to one of the city's most famous sons, Andy Payne, winner of the 1928 LA-New York marathon nicknamed the "Bunion Derby."

Much of its course lay along Route 66, and a statue commemorating Payne's victory can be seen on the left of the highway as it passes through town.

To the north of the road is Oologah Lake; Will Rogers was born near the little town on its banks that shares its name. Oologah can be reached by turning off onto SR 88 near Claremore, the great man's adopted home. 66 passes directly through Claremore, whose most famous Rogers-related site, the hotel bearing his name on the corner of Lynn Riggs Boulevard and Will Rogers Boulevard, opened in 1930, five years before his death. It attracted a string of eminent guests over the following decades, but since closing in 1991, it has been converted into retirement apartments; sadly, it now retains little of its former grandeur.

Lynn Riggs (1899–1954), another Claremore notable whose name is commemorated by a road in the town, was the author of *Green Grow The Lilacs*, the play on which Richard Rodgers and Oscar Hammerstein II based their classic musical *Oklahoma!* (1943). A Riggs memorial exhibition is on permanent display at the old library building on Weenonah Street; among the featured artifacts is the "surrey with the fringe on top" that appeared in the *Oklahoma!* movie.

Above and right: Today, The Will Rogers Hotel no longer provides Claremore's "welcome to the world," although the building (now closed to the public) is still a striking downtown landmark, and retains some of its original features.

73

OKLAHOMA

| Catoosa | 0731 | Sapulpa | 0750 | Bristow | 0800 | Luther | 0828 | Oklahoma City |
| 0714 | Tulsa | 0741 | Kellyville | 0768 | Chandler | 0819 | Arcadia | 084 |

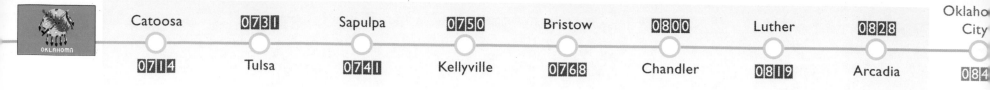

CHANDLER, OKLA.

Above: Chandler's Lincoln County Courthouse and surrounding streets. This panoramic "postcard on a roll" dates from the 1920s.

Far right: Catoosa's 80-foot (24m) Blue Whale was created in the early 1970s by local resident Hugh Davis.

AUTHORIZED   DEALER

MOTOR HARLEY-DAVIDSON CYCLES

TULSA MOTORCYCLE CO.
643 WEST 11th HI 66
TULSA, OKLAHOMA
SALES and SERVICE

Above: A sign from a Tulsa Harley-Davidson dealership; these classic motorcycles are considered by many to be the "kings of the road."

The most impressive of all the Will Rogers sites in this area is undoubtedly his Memorial, opened in 1938, and comprising an eight-gallery museum (augmented in 1982 by a new East Wing) framing the Rogers family tomb, which is set in a sunken garden. In the 1990s, the museum was extensively refurbished; it contains a library, a comprehensive archive of Rogers' personal papers and photographs, and a wide range of other exhibits. The Memorial, set in 20 acres (8ha) of surrounding grounds, is maintained by voluntary contributions, and admission is free.

After crossing the Verdigris River outside Claremore, 66 heads for Catoosa, passing the pond containing the recently renovated Blue Whale – the centerpiece of a once popular swimming and picnicing area that has now fallen into disuse. Two miles (3km) beyond the town, SR 66 meets I-44, and travelers can either use the Interstate to bypass the nearby city of Tulsa, or explore the former "Oil Capital of the World" by taking a downtown exit.

Tulsa's oil is gone, but it remains a flourishing metropolis (the second largest in the state). Several familiar landmarks on the path of the Old Road through the city, including the Will Rogers Theatre and Will Rogers Motor Court, have disappeared over the years. However, some striking recent

architecture and art can be seen on the Oral Roberts University campus (South Lewis Avenue), with its 200-foot (60m) Prayer Tower, and 40-foot (12m) tall bronze "Healing Hands" sculpture.

To resume the journey west, follow signs to Sapulpa and return to SR 66. The road continues past old oil towns like Kellyville and Bristow, where several long-abandoned alignments of 66 can be seen and (sometimes) driven down. Beyond Bristow

> ## " I never met a man I didn't like. "
>
> *Inscription on statue of Will Rogers, Will Rogers Memorial,*
> *Claremore, Oklahoma*

lies Chandler, county seat for the surrounding area; in 1897, the city was rebuilt in brick after being destroyed by a tornado. From here, it is a 28-mile (45km) drive to Arcadia, via Luther.

Right: Oklahoma City is served by a complex network of modern highways – but some traces of the Old Road still survive in this area.

Round Barn

Below: *Arcadia's Round Barn, seen from Route 66. The plaque (**inset right**) detailing the building's history is mounted on the roadside opposite.*

Arcadia's most famous landmark, its Round Barn, was built from locally grown burr oak by William Harrison Odor, a farmer and storeowner, in 1898; it is 60 feet (18m) in diameter, with a dome rising to a height of 43 feet (13m). There are two stories: a ground floor designed to shelter animals; and a loft, nine feet (3m) up, originally intended for hay and grain. However, from early in its existence, the barn was also used for dances and concerts; according to one source, the first of these were held by Mr. Odor himself to raise money for the timber flooring!

By the 1980s, the barn, which had been placed on the National Register of Historic Places in 1977, was in serious need of repairs. These began in 1988 under the auspices of the Arcadia Historical and Preservation Society, and with the blessing of the Vrana family, who had inherited the property from William. Odor many years before. Much of the work was carried out by a group of volunteers known affectionately as the "Over the Hill Gang," as they were all senior citizens. Led by a retired building contractor from Oklahoma City, Luther Robison, they rebuilt the roof and gradually restored the Round Barn to its former glory. On April 4, 1992, the renovated structure was opened to the public; later that year, the Arcadia Historical and Preservation Society received an award from the National Preservation Trust for their successful campaign to save it.

Today, the Round Barn is one of the most frequently visited sites on Route 66. On April 26, 1998, special celebrations were held to mark its centenary; these included a vintage automobile show and an exhibition of paintings by Oklahoma artists. The barn has also become a popular venue for social events, meetings – and even weddings.

Left: Ralph Odor and Hesper Williams, descendants of William Harrison Odor, inspect the dilapidated barn in 1976.
Above: The building as it is today.

| | 0800 | Luther | 0828 | Oklahoma City | 0853 | El Reno | 0874 | Geary |
| OKLAHOMA | Chandler | 0819 | Arcadia | 0842 | Yukon | 0866 | Calumet | 0886 |

O klahoma City was formed during the Land Rush of 1889, when a huge influx of claim-stakers settled in an area then known as Oklahoma Station. Within months of its formation, this community, which soon numbered over 10,000 and continued to grow rapidly, had appointed civic officials and set up a local Commercial Club. It was already a major center for business and railroad transportation by the time Oklahoma achieved statehood in 1907, but did not replace Guthrie, about 30 miles (48km) to the north, as state capital until 1910. Today, it is home to more than a million people – about a third of the entire population of Oklahoma.

Above: Downtown Yukon – a flour mill and the Farmers' Co-Op stand on either side of Route 66, which forms the city's Main Street.

Above: This statue of Buffalo Bill (William Frederick Cody, 1846–1917) stands on Oklahoma City's Persimmon Hill, near the National Cowboy and Western Heritage Museum.
Above top: Meiki's Route 66 Restaurant lies on the 39th Street Expressway (SR66) in OKC.

Geographically, the OKC area lies on the edge of the Great Plains region, where, in the words of Bob Waldmire, who has spent many years traveling, drawing, and mapping the Old Road, "the land begins to 'open up' [as] the forests give way to broad expanses of rolling grasslands." The highway has been climbing steadily over the last 150 miles (240km); OKC is almost 2000 feet (610m) above sea level, and the road continues its gradual ascent as it heads west.

I-44 enters the city north of the downtown area; above the highway, on Persimmon Hill, is the National Cowboy Hall of Fame & Western Heritage Center (NE 63rd Street), which features a wide range of displays, portraits, statues, and memorabilia. Other attractions, including the Capitol complex on North Lincoln Boulevard, are also easily accessible from 44, which turns south a few miles later. At this point (exit 123A) we join the 39th Street Expressway (SR 66), which passes the 66 Bowl (the oldest bowling alley in OKC) and a number of motels and other buildings that recall the glory days of Route 66. The road leads through the suburb of Bethany, past Lake Overholser, and on towards Yukon.

· VOICE OF THE ROAD ·

E. Tolly Clymer

E. Tolly Clymer, of Oklahoma City, had a long career as a Greyhound bus driver. He trained in Springfield, Missouri, qualified in 1935, and moved to Oklahoma a year later. His arrival in OKC coincided with the introduction of the first metal-bodied Greyhounds – whose improved insulation was a boon for drivers and passengers accustomed to the older wooden vehicles. The shiver in Clymer's voice is unmistakable as he recalls, during an interview for the Oklahoma Historical Society, "driving those things in the winters I spent in Missouri."

Clymer goes on to explain that "at that time the Greyhound lines were broken down into 12 or 14 small companies, and the region through here was known as the southwestern Greyhound line". He and his colleagues (many of them former teachers and "professional" men attracted by the good rates of pay) operated throughout Oklahoma, Texas, Arkansas, Missouri, Kansas, New Mexico, and Colorado. During this period, there was real camaraderie between drivers and regular passengers; Clymer himself met his future wife on the bus, and, while describing the special appeal of his job, comments that "the road was a part of it, as well as the people."

Right: *For decades, OKC has been an important staging post for Greyhound and other long-distance bus companies.*

Left: *The 66 Bowl offers customers week-long sport, food, and drink; and on Saturday nights it becomes what its owners call "OKC's rockinest place for live music."*

66 BOWL

Snack BAR LOUNGE

NOV 6
THE POISON OKIES
FEATURING
MACK STEVENS

ARCADE Pro SHOP

79

Below: A World War Two bomber aircraft standing by the roadside in front of El Reno's VFW (Veterans of Foreign Wars) Post.

Above: Low water on the South Canadian River – the view downstream from the bridge on US 281 shown in the main picture (see right).

Yukon lies on the path of the old Chisholm Trail – the cattle-driving route, named for trader Jesse Chisholm (1805–1868), that once stretched from Texas to Kansas. The little town had only 81 inhabitants when it was established in 1891, but it flourished when the Choctaw, Oklahoma and Gulf railroad built its tracks there just a few months later. Yukon subsequently became a center for flour milling from locally harvested grain, and recent building booms have helped the area retain its prosperity – despite its bypassing by I-40, which runs a little to the south.

Like Yukon, El Reno, whose Big 8 Motel was featured in Dustin Hoffman's *Rain Man* (although the movie itself is set in Amarillo), benefited from the railroad as well as the highway. It also has strong military associations: nearby Fort Reno was set up in 1874 as a cavalry outpost, and also served as a "remount" station, where riders would change horses on long journeys; during World War II it housed a POW camp. Its historic buildings have been preserved and are open to visitors.

The road beyond Fort Reno includes a rougher, unpaved stretch. Beyond it, near Calumet, take US 270, which leads to Geary; then turn left onto US 281 and continue south to Bridgeport, crossing the South Canadian River near the town. From here, the road leads west to Hydro – site of the famous service station run by Lucille Hamons, whose fascinating stories and reminiscences of life on 66 are featured in her autobiography *Lucille: Mother of the Mother Road*. The station opened in the 1940s, and Lucille remained there until her death on August 18, 2000.

Clinton, about 22 miles (35km) down the highway, is also rich in memories of Route 66's golden years, as we shall see on the following pages.

Left: This vivid mural, on the side of a building at Yukon's 4th and Main, commemorates the Chisholm Trail, which played a key role in the economic development of this area.

Below: Blue skies and a clear road – looking east across the South Canadian River bridge on US 281 near Bridgeport. The water marks the boundary between Oklahoma's Canadian and Custer counties.

Above: Roughening road surface on a section of 66 near Fort Reno.

> **Route 66 was more than just a ribbon of concrete running from Chicago to California; it was the Highway of Dreams. It was Route 66 to a second chance, a new beginning. It was the route you took to start over.**
>
> *from* Incident on Sixth Street *by D.R. Meredith, 1999*

Left: The New Motel, near 9th and Main, Yukon, is located just a few doors down from the Yukon Motel shown on page 67. Both establishments share a similar taste for impressively outsize illuminated signs!

81

Luther		Oklahoma City		El Reno		Geary	
0828		0853		0874		0894	
0819	Arcadia	0842	Yukon	0866	Calumet	0886	Bridgeport

Right: The Calmez Hotel, Frisco Street, Clinton – a perfect example of what 66 expert Bob Waldmire describes as the city's "relict architecture."

Below: The Trading Post Restaurant, Custer City, lies east of Clinton on I-40. It is a particular favorite with truckers – the most discerning and knowledgeable consumers of road food!

Among Clinton's many attractions is the Route 66 Museum at 2229 Gary Boulevard. Set up in 1995 under the auspices of the Oklahoma Historical Society, it contains a remarkable collection of exhibits and displays reflecting every period of the highway's existence; artifacts on show include tools used by early road builders, original maps, photographs, posters, and even vehicles!

Sadly, though, not everything associated with the Old Road in Clinton can be preserved for posterity. One famous downtown landmark, Pop Hicks Restaurant, which had been providing sustenance to travelers since 1936, was severely damaged by fire in August 1999, and is now closed. However, other long-established local businesses continue to thrive, like the Glancy Motor Hotel next door to the ruins of Pop Hicks; and there are plans to renovate the old Calmez Hotel on Third and Frisco, which dates from 1929.

Right: This pretty roadside sign once attracted customers to the now boarded-up Cotton Boll Motel in Canute.

Far right: Kobel's Place, Foss – a fading, long-abandoned building in a settlement that has now become a ghost town.

Route 66 continues its journey west, running close to I-40. Fifteen miles (24km) from Clinton is the small, almost deserted settlement of Foss – a busier place during the World War II years, when there was a naval base nearby. Canute, a little further down the road, is most notable for the impressive statues and grotto in its Holy Family Catholic cemetery on the eastern side of the town, and for its elevation – at 1910 feet (582m) above sea level, it is the highest point on 66 so far. As Michael Wallis observes in his *Route 66: The Mother Road*, "the land [here] is rolling and hilly…[and] the Oklahoma soil is its deepest red at this point."

From Canute, it is just six miles (10km) to Elk City – originally named Busch after Adolphus Busch (1839–1913) of the famous Busch–Anheuser brewery, but rechristened after the newly formed state of Oklahoma banned the sale of alcohol in 1907. 66 leads us directly into the heart of town.

POP HICKS RESTAURANT

Tom Snyder, in his Route 66 Traveler's Guide, *described Pop Hicks Restaurant as "like a town bulletin board with silverware." Situated at 223 Gary Boulevard, it was as popular with local residents as with travelers. Despite its international fame (at one stage, its menu even appeared on the Internet) it never lost its distinctive atmosphere or its reputation for traditional, satisfying food.*

Pop Hicks changed hands many times in its 63-year life; its most recent owners were Howard Nichols – an Old Road catering veteran, who had run a drive-in restaurant in Amarillo until the arrival of the Interstate – and his wife Mary. After acquiring it in 1989, they provided 24-hour service, and offered their customers classic dishes like Cook's Shack Chicken Wings, steakburgers, and Funks Grove Peach Cobbler. Sadly, though, even Howard's energy and commitment could not keep this famous landmark open after the devastating fire that engulfed it in 1999, shortly after his wife's death.

ROUTE
66

Indian Chief

Indian planned to capitalize on the post-war boom in motorcycle ownership with bikes that would appeal to homecoming GIs, many of whom had bought lighter British-made machines while serving in Europe. But its new designs proved inferior to the classic Chief and Scout models.

The Indian Motorcycle Company sprang from a collaboration between engineer Oscar Hedstrom and businessman George Hendee, who started producing single-cylinder bikes at a small factory in Springfield, Massachusetts in 1902. The firm grew rapidly, and its innovative designs (which included the 1913 Hendee Special, the first-ever machine with an electric start system) enjoyed international success. By 1914, Indian had established itself as the biggest motorcycle maker in the world, and had swept the board at American and European racing events, including the prestigious UK Isle of Man TT competition, where it won first, second and third prizes in 1912.

EAST TEXAS-OKLAHOMA
WITH
NEW MEXICO-WEST TEXAS

TEXACO
REG.T.M.

PAPER IS PRECIOUS!
Please do not throw
this map away

THE DEALER WHO GIVES YOU THIS MAP CAN
GET YOU THE MOST COMFORTABLE ROUTING
FOR ANY TRIP ANYWHERE IN CANADA, MEXICO
AND THE UNITED STATES

Above: This Texaco road map dates from the 1940s; its reminder that "paper is precious" reflects the climate of austerity during the war years, when Americans were encouraged to avoid waste. One famous poster campaign of the period popularized the slogan "If You Don't Need It, Don't Buy It."

The steel-framed Chief has a 61in (155cm) wheelbase and weighs 560lb (254kg).

Over the following decades, Indian survived the departure of its founders and a period of uncertain management, exacerbated by the effects of the Depression, and went on to supply thousands of machines to the US Army in World War Two. However, delays to plans for a new range of lightweight designs meant that by 1947 the firm had just one model in production: its classic V-twin Chief. This was temporarily discontinued the following year, when Indian launched a range of smaller single- and twin-cylinder machines; but these proved unsuccessful, and the Chief was eventually restored to the catalog in 1950.

Above: The Chief could reach a top speed of 85mph (137kph); on this machine the original speedometer (made by Stewart-Warner) has been replaced by a 1952 Corbin speedo, while the ammeter dates from 1947.

This splendid 1948 Indian Chief has been restored by its present owner, Bob Stark of Perris, California.

Priced at $475, the Indian Chief was a popular machine – but was easily outsold by models from the company's competitors, notably Harley-Davidson.

The old Parker Drilling Company rig sited beside Route 66 on Elk City's 3rd Street is a reminder of this area's history as an oil and gas supplier. Today, the town is flourishing, although its economy suffered a severe blow in 1974, when the newly opened Interstate began to divert traffic and customers away from the Old Road. Wanda Queenan, who set up Queenan's Indian Trading Post, specializing in Native American curios, on the west side of Elk City in 1948, struggled to keep her store open through this difficult period. As she explains in an oral history recording made by the Oklahoma Historical Society, "I missed the tourists, unless it would be someone who had been there

GAS 9 3/10
S.F. TAX 4 1/2
TOTAL 13 8/10

MAGNOLIA GASOLINE

Above: An oil derrick in action at the roadside between Elk City and Sayre.

Left: Elk City's National Route 66 Museum mimics the appearance of various Old Road-style buildings.
Far left: A vintage pump positioned next to the museum's "gas station" façade (right hand section of frontage).

Left: "Buffalo on the Prairie" statue by Joe E. Smith of Leedey, OK (1999), sited just east of the Route 66 Museum.

Below: Elk City's Old Town Museum area features a wide variety of interesting exhibits and recreated buildings – like the "opera house" shown here.
Bottom: This caboose (at the roadside nearby) can be boarded by visitors.

several times and knew where to find me." In 1980, Wanda was forced to close: "I just [had to] quit buying from the Indians because I didn't have an outlet for their work. The road is a different thing today than what it was."

However, Wanda Queenan did not abandon Elk City. She is now curator of its National Route 66 Museum, based in the central Old Town Museum complex. The 66 Museum's entrance is flanked by the Kachina doll that once stood guard outside her trading post; inside, visitors can enjoy a wide range of exhibits associated with the road, including a series of murals and "vignettes" illustrating locations from each of the states it passes through. Nearby, other museums celebrate the achievements of pioneers, farmers and ranchers; and there are also a number of outdoor artifacts associated with the Old Town – including a wigwam, and an old Choctaw, Oklahoma, and Gulf caboose commemorating the first railroad line to link Elk City with El Reno. Admission tickets can be bought for individual museums, or for the entire site.

Below: Just follow that sign...one of several colorful murals to be seen on 4th Street in Sayre. What lies beyond the padlocked stockade?

E lk City and the next staging post on our journey, Sayre, both lie in the heart of Western Oklahoma's Anadarko Basin, a geological region rich in oil and natural gas deposits; occasionally, active derricks can be seen by the roadside. Sayre itself has another claim to distinction; it is known as the "Cradle of the Quarterhorse" – a compact, powerful equine breed originally intended for quarter-mile racing – and there are a number of sizeable ranches nearby.

Near the town, 66 crosses the north fork of the Red River – once considered by Texas to be the state line, until a 1896 Supreme Court decision ruled otherwise. Practically nothing remains of Hext, about eight miles (13km) further down the road. Jack D. Rittenhouse, in his 1946 guide, remarked that it was "not a community – just a gas station," adding wryly (and with some justice), that "from here on west many of the 'towns' shown on usual road maps often contain no more than one

Above: Water Hole #2, Texola, with its curious, faintly sinister decor (note the birds of prey on the wall paintings) and slumbering canine guard.

Above right: A disused section of road near Hext.
Right: The view from just across the state line, where westbound Route 66 (in the foreground) runs parallel to the east and westbound lanes of I-40.

> " 66 is the path of a people in flight, refugees from dust and shrinking land, from the thunder of tractors and shrinking ownership, from the desert's slow northward invasion, from the twisting winds that howl up out of Texas, from the floods that bring no richness to the land and steal what little richness is there. From all of these the people are in flight, and they come into 66 from the tributary side roads, from the wagon tracks and the rutted country roads. 66 is the mother road, the road of flight. "

from The Grapes of Wrath *by John Steinbeck, 1939*

building." Erick, another eight miles (13km) from here, is a more substantial place with a small footnote in popular music history: it was the birthplace of both Roger Miller, singer and composer of "King of the Road," and Sheb Wooley of "Purple People Eater" fame.

We now reach the border town of Texola – once a thriving little community, but now a ghostly shadow of its former self, due to the coming of the Interstate, which passes just to the north. A few buildings, two bars (one derelict and covered in bizarre graffiti), and some abandoned vehicles are all that survive; and the small number of cars and trucks that still pass through do little to disturb the surrounding stillness – or the slumber of the dog resting outside "Water Hole #2." Just west of here, we leave the Sooner State behind and enter Wheeler County, Texas.

Signs

Below: An illuminated Route 66 shield adorns the roof of the 66 Diner at 1405 Central Avenue, Albuquerque, NM.

The "Route 66" shield, the most famous sign associated with the Old Road, was introduced in the 1920s, when major thoroughfares were reclassified either as US highways (with shield markers) or state roads (with circular signs). The distinctive shield helped drivers find their way along the largely unpaved new east-west route, and several roadside businesses, from "Phillips 66" gasoline to individual stores and motels, later incorporated it on their own billboards and logos.

They had plenty of opportunities to display these. Advertising on Route 66 was relatively unregulated; and with nothing to prevent the erection of signs and posters on private land adjacent to the highway, traders could develop ingenious ways of attracting passing motorists' attention. Some publicity campaigns used a series of displays to repeatedly "plug" a location or service. Lester Dill, manager of the Meramec Caverns site near Stanton, Missouri, was a master of this method. From the 1930s onwards, he covered roadside barns for hundreds of miles around with signs promoting the caves; as he told

Below: Painted barns like these have been used for decades to advertise Missouri's famous Meramec Caverns.

Left: One of the many distinctive highway-side billboards promoting the Jack Rabbit Trading Post in Joseph City, AZ.

Below: Part of a sequence of Burma Shave signs. The next three boards read LET FOLKS SEE/HOW BRIGHT/<u>YOU</u> ARE.

Left: Burma Shave signs in miniature – a Cat's Meow Village model of the celebrated red-and-white roadside placards.

Susan Croce Kelly, "Every time I painted a barn, my pocketbook would get fatter and fatter. Those barns really done the trick."

The famous Burma Shave ads, introduced in 1926, were more subtle: a series of witty jingles, displayed, line by line and exactly 100 paces apart, on a succession of distinctively colored signs. The campaign was immediately popular, and ran until the company was sold in the early 1960s.

By then, the old free and easy attitude to roadside hoardings had changed. Unregulated advertising was prohibited on the Interstates, and in 1965, the passage of the Highway Beautification Act (strongly supported by Ladybird Johnson, the President's wife) gave the government powers to remove many of the signs that had been so effective in attracting trade to Route 66.

Above: Even the most commonplace signs associated with the Old Road have now become treasured relics; the two examples seen here are preserved at the Route 66 Visitor Center in Hackberry, AZ.

Left: This cryptic message adorns the wall of an old beer hall in Texola, OK.

Texas

The route taken by 66 and I-40 across the Texas Panhandle leads through the starkly impressive "staked plains;" as Jack D. Rittenhouse commented in 1946, "the newcomer to this region is impressed with the almost limitless emptiness of the countryside." Beyond Amarillo lies what Rittenhouse describes as "the true west," and at Adrian, 23miles (37km) from the border with New Mexico, we reach the halfway point on our journey.

Above: The Texas State flag. Its design was adopted in 1839: the red, white, and blue colors symbolize (respectively) courage, strength, and loyalty.
Main picture: The "Leaning Water Tower of Texas." This oddly angled landmark stands on the outskirts of Groom, about 40 miles (64km) east of Amarillo.

Texas

Below: A souvenir model of Shamrock's famous Tower gas station and U-Drop Inn.
Below right: The desolate stretch of road near the Jericho Gap between Alanreed and Groom.

According to Michael Wallis' *Route 66: The Mother Road*, "the first Panhandle roads were marked by furrows, plowed into the prairie soil." Travel was made easier by the arrival of the railroad at the start of the 20th century; nearly all the settlements on the path of 66 in Texas owe their existence to the Chicago, Rock Island and Gulf Railway, whose line west to Glenrio was completed by 1906.

Route 66 was officially opened two decades later; however, in Texas (and further west), parts of it remained unpaved for years afterwards. In some areas, it was impossible even to gain access to the road: as late as 1930, according to one witness (quoted in Susan Croce Kelly's *Route 66*), four wire gates were blocking the still ungraded highway between Shamrock and Amarillo. Travelers could not be guaranteed a clear path across Texas's 180

miles (290km) of 66 until concreting was completed in the late 1930s.

Even with a paved surface, driving on the Old Road could often be hazardous, due to the alarmingly changeable weather conditions sometimes encountered in the Panhandle. In his *Guide Book to Highway 66*, Jack D. Rittenhouse describes the fierce winds that "bring sudden temperature drops and sometimes whip up clouds of sand;" and former Greyhound bus driver Howard Suttle's *Behind the Wheel…On Route 66* includes this vivid account of being caught in a Spring blizzard near Groom. "We found lines of traffic stalled on both the east and west lanes of Route 66…the snow was only about six inches deep, but it was very wet and heavy, accompanied by a high wind…The tall grain elevators could be seen once in a while at Groom, but…it might

Right: This bizarre sign, advertising a snakefarm, can be seen from I-40 a few miles east of McLean.

Right: Waterbags were once an essential item for travelers on 66.

as well have been a hundred miles [away] under these circumstances: we just couldn't get there." Suttle and his passengers remained stranded on the blocked highway for more than 24 hours.

Thankfully, conditions like these are unusual. Driving this section of the road is normally straightforward and trouble-free, and it is only necessary to resort to the Interstate on three or four occasions. The journey through Texas can easily be completed in a few hours; but it is well worth taking more time to explore the little towns on 66's path, and perhaps making an overnight stop in Amarillo, which offers excellent food and accommodation.

Below: Livestock remains vital to the Texas economy – and the sight of cowboys at work is a major tourist attraction for visitors to Amarillo.

Above: An abandoned café and gas station on the northern frontage of Route 66 at Wildorado.
Below: Phillips 66 gas was not actually named after the Old Road, but its distinctive shield is still a familiar sight.

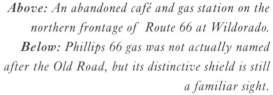

95

Cadillac Fleetwood

The outrageously elevated "zap" fins on the 1959 Cadillacs attracted criticism and ridicule from some commentators; they were much less prominent on later models, and were dropped after 1964.

Cadillac produced its first car in the early 1900s, when engine maker Henry Leland joined forces with some ex-Ford staffers in Detroit to create the Model A, a two-seater, single-cylinder vehicle selling for $750. Cadillac was named for the French pioneer, Antoine de la Mothe Cadillac (1658–1730), who founded the city of Detroit in 1701; his crest has been a company trademark since 1906. From its earliest years, Cadillac has focused on excellence

Below: The elegant shaping of the Fleetwood's rear window echoes the more dramatic wraparound design of its front windshield.

The Cadillac Fleetwood is over 18 feet (5700mm) long, with a wheelbase of 10ft 10in (3302mm), and one of the largest trunk spaces created for any car of this type.

and luxury, and is also a byword for striking body design: Harley Earl, who set up the General Motors "Art and Color" section in 1927, and worked there until his retirement more than 30 years later, was responsible for innovations like the introduction of Cadillac's famous tail fins in 1948. Over the following years, these grew in size and prominence, reaching their apotheosis in the company's 1959 models - like the Fleetwood shown here, whose other hallmarks (quadruple headlights, front and rear grilles decorated with chromium-plated bullets, and projectile-like rear lights) all enhance its bold image. The car's powerful V8 engine ensures that its performance matches its looks.

Below: These quadruple headlamps were also featured on the previous year's Cadillac Eldorados.

The Fleetwood's luxurious interior design featured individually adjustable front seats.

Below: The luxurious interior can be seen through its tinted windshield. To the left of the steering wheel is an "Autronic Eye" – an optional extra that sensed the lights of oncoming cars and dipped the car's headlights

Right: Gas consumption on the Fleetwood was predictably heavy; the car would manage little more than 14 miles to the gallon (20lit/100km).

SINCLAIR H-C GASOLINE

Below: Shamrock's Art Deco-influenced U-Drop Inn and Tower gas station date from 1936. The two adjoining businesses were ideally positioned to serve travelers on both Route 66 and US 83.

As we leave the rich Oklahoma scenery behind, and begin our 180-mile (290km) journey across the Panhandle, Route 66 runs alongside I-40 as a frontage road, and the terrain continues its gradual rise. Fifteen miles (24km) from the border is the town of Shamrock. Originally the name given in 1890 "for good luck and courage" to a dugout home owned by an Irish settler, George Nickel (or Nichols), Shamrock subsequently became a stop on the Chicago, Rock Island and Gulf Railway, which

arrived in the area in 1902. Over the following decades, the town developed into a thriving industrial center, and the discovery of oil nearby in 1926 gave a further boost to its population and prosperity.

When the stretch of Route 66 running through Shamrock was concreted in 1938, the town's bandmaster, Glen Truax, decided to mark the occasion with a St. Patrick's Day parade. This custom, involving a weekend of celebrations, has continued ever since; and Shamrock's Celtic connections have also been enhanced by its acquisition, in 1959, of a piece of the Blarney Stone – taken from Blarney Castle, near Cork in Eire, and supposed to endow those who kiss it with special powers of persuasion. Visitors can put this legend to

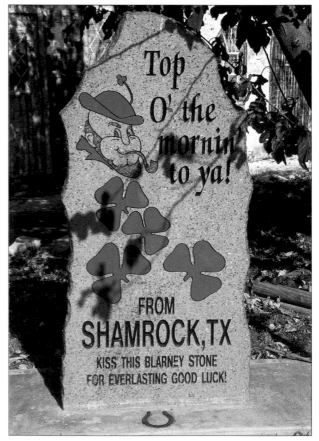

Above: A touch of the Emerald Isle deep in the heart of Texas. This engraved stone can be seen in the "Irish Village" on Shamrock's Main Street.

Right: The U-Drop's owner, John Nunn, is said to have sketched its outline in the roadside dust with a nail! The building's construction took two years and cost a princely $23,000.

the test by seeking out the Stone in Shamrock's Elmore City Park; there is also an "Irish Village" on the town's Main Street.

Shamrock lies on both Route 66 and the Canada–Mexico highway, US 83; in April 1936, the Art Deco-style U-Drop Inn (christened by a local eight-year old boy who won a competition to find a name for the new restaurant) and Tower gas station were opened at the intersection of the two thoroughfares. They became key landmarks on the Old Road as well as popular stopping places for food and gas, but are now closed to customers.

Above: Heading west…the view from a bridge over I-40 at exit 169, a few miles outside Shamrock.
Above left: A piece of the authentic Blarney Stone, obtained from Ireland in 1959 and now on display in Shamrock's Elmore City Park.

*Left: A small **oil** derrick operating by the roadside on the north frontage of Route 66, west of Texola, near the Oklahoma / Texas border.*

Right: This tiny Phillips 66 gas station on McLean's First Street dates from the 1930s, and has recently been restored.

Above: The Devil's Rope Museum, Kingsley Street, McLean. The twin barbed wire balls featured in the "tribute" displayed outside the building were contributed by Frank and Violet Smith of Keller, near Dallas.

Lela, just west of Shamrock, was created by the coming of the railroad in the early 1900s, but soon overshadowed by its larger neighbors. Fifteen miles (24km) beyond it lies McLean, which, like Shamrock, owed much of its original prosperity to an oilstrike in the 1920s, and to the advent of Route 66 at about the same time. During World War II, the town's population of 1500 was boosted by some temporary, involuntary residents – German prisoners-of-war based at a camp east of the town, who would occasionally earn themselves 80 cents a day working on local ranches or as street sweepers.

Today, McLean is a more sparsely inhabited, sleepier place, but it still contains much to attract and intrigue visitors – including the Devil's Rope Museum, devoted to the history of barbed wire, an invention that played a key part in the settling of the West. Over 1000 different types are on show, alongside tools, photos and other exhibits. The museum is sited on Kingsley Street, in a building once occupied by a Sears brassiere factory.

Alanreed, the next little town on the path of 66, was established in 1900, and named for the two partners in the firm that laid it out. In the old days,

1013	Bushland	1125	Vega	1152	Glenrio	1175	Endee	1189
Cadillac Ranch	1016	Wildorado	1138	Adrian	1175	Glenrio	1180	Bard

· VOICE OF THE ROAD ·

Frank Swindel

Texan-born Frank Swindel has fascinating memories of his life as a truck driver on Route 66. As he explains in an interview for the Oklahoma Historical Society, he started working for the Leeway Freight Company at the age of 16, in 1944: "They didn't really have a training program – they sent you on a trip with a senior driver, and he was the one who'd tell [the boss] OK or not." Swindel made the grade, and later graduated to the "hot-shot" delivery service: an express run, which, in the early 1950s, made use of the only diesel-powered trucks in the Leeway fleet. He recalls that "a man would leave Oklahoma City about 1 or 2 o'clock in the afternoon to go to Tulsa, and he would deliver some stuff – whatever was real rushed, some kind of special thing." Swindel also took part in overnight deliveries to Amarillo, and occasionally handled "security" loads supervised by the FBI: "You didn't know what you was hauling for sure... but there were three Federal officers following in a car, [and they] didn't let the trailer out of their sight."

Above: 66 forms McLean's First Street – and this elegantly evocative mural can be seen downtown at the Old Road's junction with Rowe.

Right: Gas pumps with odometer-style dials, like this classic Phillips 66 model, were in wide use on filling station forecourts by the mid-1930s.

there was little love lost between its residents and their neighbors from McLean. According to Michael Wallis, in his *Route 66 – The Mother Road*, an incident when a local wrangler attempted to tear out the eyes of a man from McLean in a bar fight led to Alanreed being nicknamed "Gouge Eye." Bob Moore and Patrick Grauwels' *Illustrated Guidebook to the Mother Road* has a different version of the story, in which the "eyeballs" are merely grapes, and the lurid account of the gouging is made up by drinkers to alarm a passing stranger!

Gas stations

Below: "66" Super Service Station, (with a Texaco pump on its forecourt) built in downtown Alanreed, TX, by Bradley Kiser in 1930.

Opposite (clockwise from top): Standard Oil gas station, displaying the famous Chevron emblem ("as old as heraldry and as honorable as knighthood," in the words of the company's publicity) introduced in 1931; a mule train passes a Mobilgas outlet in downtown Winslow, AZ; the Route 66 Visitor Center in Hackberry, AZ, with its splendid collection of gas station artifacts; one of the inspection teams despatched by Union 76 to check out the cleanliness of its restrooms; a Texaco attendant cuts ice cubes for his customers; and a 1929 postcard of a Texaco station in Two Guns, AZ.

Gas stations were the first and most essential of all Route 66's roadside businesses. The oldest one still standing on the highway, the Soulsby Shell Station at Mount Olive, Illinois, was built in 1926 by Henry Soulsby and his son Russell. At 13 feet by 20 feet (4m by 6m), its original premises were smaller than the restrooms in most modern facilities; it was enlarged during the 1930s, and the Soulsby family continued to operate it until 1991.

In the early days of 66, many stations were still in private hands, like Soulsby's. But major gas suppliers soon saw the advantages of controlling their own outlets; their growing wealth enabled them to invest in premium locations, expand the range of services on offer, and create a distinctive, instantly recognizable image for their brands. One firm, Phillips, which began selling gas in 1927, even adapted the Route 66 shield for its logo, and christened its fuel "Phillips 66." There are several conflicting stories about the origins of the name. According to Michael Karl Witzel, writing in *Route 66 Magazine*, it was chosen after a company official commented to his driver, while on the road near Tulsa, that "This car goes like sixty on our new gas!" "Sixty nothing," replied the driver, "We're doing 66!"

Phillips, Mobil, Texaco and other key suppliers all had a significant presence on the Old Road; but there were also opportunities for independent oil companies. One of the most successful of these was Whiting Bros., an Arizona-based firm that favored cheap, out-of-town sites for its stations, and provided cut-price fuel throughout the western states from Texas to California. Sadly, like so many smaller companies, Whiting Bros. lost the bulk of its trade when the Interstates diverted long-distance traffic away from its outlets, and it was forced to close in 1985.

Below: One of Amarillo's most famous eateries, the Big Texan Steak Ranch Restaurant, whose menu includes a 72oz. steak dinner offered free to any customer who can consume it in less than an hour!

Right: A cattle auction in progress in downtown Amarillo. The city is a long-established regional center for the livestock trade.

Above: The period-style exterior of the Big Texan Motel, adjacent to the restaurant. Its rooms also have a Western look and feel, with fixtures and fitings such as cow-horn lamps and saloon-type doors.

Beyond Alanreed, 66's tarmac surface disappears, and it soon becomes impossible to continue west along it. Travelers may be disappointed at having to take I-40 for the next few miles, but should reflect that the vanished stretch of Old Road was part of the so-called "Jericho Gap," infamous in the highway's early days for its "gumbo soil" – which was rock hard while dry but dangerously slippery and greasy when wet. Jericho itself can be accessed from the freeway, and west of here, it is possible to rejoin the frontage road. This leads to Groom, on whose eastern edge stands the "Leaning Tower of Texas" – a slanting water tower that is one of the most frequently photographed landmarks on the Old Road. The name

| 1113 | | Bushland | | 1125 | | Vega | | 1152 | | Glenrio | ¦ | 1175 | | Endee | | 1189 |
| Cadillac Ranch | | 1116 | | Wildorado | | 1138 | | Adrian | | 1175 | ¦ | Glenrio | | 1180 | | Bard |

Below: A herd of prime Texas cattle waiting to be despatched to auction from this stockyard near Amarillo.

" Pretty soon another cattle man offered me a ride on to the next cattle town. He smoked a pipe which had took up more of his time in the last twenty years than wife, kids, or his cow ranching. He told me, 'This old Panhandle country can be one mighty nice place when it's purty, but hell on wheels when she gits riled up! "

from Bound For Glory *by Woody Guthrie, 1943*

"Britten," displayed on the structure, belongs to a local family that constitutes about 10 percent of the little town's population.

By now, we have climbed to over 3000 feet (915m) above sea level, and are in the midst of what Jack D. Rittenhouse describes as "a treeless, flat plain, [on which] US 66 lies straight as a dropped arrow" – a landscape that will change little until we are well into New Mexico. The highway continues through Conway and towards Amarillo – the only substantial city on 66 in Texas, which retains its cowboy roots but owes much of its current prosperity to helium production – about 90 percent of the world's supply of the gas comes from this region.

Visitors to Amarillo will find it hard to resist the prospect of a meal in one of the city's excellent restaurants, which include the Big Texan Steak Ranch (on the east of town, off I-40's Lakeside exit), and the Iron Horse Café in the old downtown railroad depot. Other places of interest include the Livestock Auction (held at Grand and Third), and the shopping area around Sixth and Western.

Above: An old, unpaved alignment of 66 near Jericho Gap. Beyond the cattle grid, the road becomes a private track leading toward a nearby ranch.

Above: The bluebonnet, Texas' offical flower, flourishes by the side of Route 66 all over the Lone Star State.

A few miles west of Amarillo is perhaps the most unusual artistic spectacle on Route 66. Cadillac Ranch, a group of ten Cadillacs buried at an angle in a field, is sited near exit 60 on the south side of I-40. (Keep a careful eye out for it, as it stands some way back from the highway.) Close examination of the cars is only possible on foot. They can be reached via a roadside gate leading onto land owned by Stanley Marsh III, a millionaire art connoisseur and longtime Amarillo resident who commissioned this "site specific" tableau from The Ant Farm – an *avant garde*, San Francisco-based collective formed by Chip Lord, Hudson B. Marquez, and Doug Michels (see sidebar). The piece was created in

Above: Cadillac Ranch, west of Amarillo.
Right: Looking southwest from the old railroad line near Bushland. Traffic on Route 66 can be seen beyond the tracks.

Above: Disused railroad tracks west of Bushland. Remnants like these are all that survive of the line that once ran parallel to Route 66 throughout this area.

1974, but has since been further embellished with spray paint and graffiti from passers-by, and was moved to its current location in 1997. The cars themselves were acquired from local scrapyards for a few hundred dollars each; the models used range from a 1949 Club Coupé to a 1964 Sedan.

Beyond Cadillac Ranch, 66 continues across the open, level landscape known by the Spanish travelers who were the first Europeans to traverse it

as the "staked plains" (*llano estacado*), after the wooden posts they used to help them find their way through this featureless terrain. Crossing over onto the northern frontage road, we pass through Bushland, a small settlement and railroad stop founded in 1908 on land donated by businessman and civic benefactor William Henry Bush (1849–1931), who played a key role in the development of the Panhandle. Never a large place, Bushland has been further diminished by the closure of the railroad (a few fragments of which can still be seen nearby) and the coming of I-40 during the 1970s.

THE ANT FARM

The Ant Farm worked together for less than 10 years; but in that time they acquired a substantial reputation for their achievements in a variety of media. Each member of the San Francisco-based group had his own special area of expertise: Chip Lord was an early exponent of experimental video; Hudson B. Marquez was an art graduate and painter; while Doug Michels had studied at Yale University College of Architecture. As successful artists with a distinctively radical approach, they quickly attracted the attention of Stanley Marsh III – a man with his own colorful and somewhat eccentric aesthetic tastes; and Cadillac Ranch, which he commissioned from the group, remains their best-known piece of work. All three members of the Ant Farm are still active on the contemporary American art scene; in 1994, they returned to the site of Cadillac Ranch for a party to mark the 20th anniversary of its creation.

Above and right: The disappearance of the railroad and the advent of the freeway have led to the closure of many roadside businesses on this stretch of 66 – including Wildorado's "Hitchin' Post Café," with its adjoining store and gas station.

ildorado, about nine miles (14km) west of Bushland, is another old railroad settlement, chiefly notable for the large stockyard that lies on 66's southern frontage. Over the years, cattle and their transportation have also been a major source of income for Vega, the next stop on the old Rock Island railroad. The town, whose name is Spanish for "plain," began to take shape in 1903, when a general store was opened there. By 1915, its population had grown to more than 200, and it had become the administrative seat for Oldham County, which incorporates much of the Western stretch of Route 66 in Texas. The University of Texas Handbook comments that "the development of

tourist courts and other facilities for travelers on US Highway 66…greatly enhanced [Vega's] economy," and the close links between the Old Road and the local community remain strong. In 1996, Vega and Adrian (about 14 miles [22km] further west) marked 66's 70th anniversary with a celebratory barbecue that attracted guests from throughout the USA; and in December 1999, when traffic throughout the region was brought to a standstill by a violent snowstorm, downtown stores were able to supply stranded motorists with the shovels, ice scrapers, and tow ropes they needed to get moving again.

Adrian has its own special significance to travelers on 66: it is generally recognized as the halfway point between Chicago and Los Angeles – although there are inevitable disputes about the precise mileages involved. The town's appropriately named Midpoint Café (featured on the next two pages) is its most famous landmark. However, visitors should also be sure not to overlook the nearby Bent Door Café, built in a style described by Tom Snyder in his *Route 66 Traveler's Guide* as "Panhandle Weird" – even though it is not currently open for business.

Below: Looking west down 66 a few miles outside Adrian. Here, the road stretches to the horizon, and only two isolated trees interrupt the desolate expanse of the Panhandle landscape.

Below: Yet another local variation on the famous "Route 66" shield. In recent years, federal funds have been provided to improve signposting and surfacing on the Old Road.

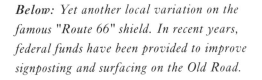

Right: The "Panhandle Weird" exterior of the Bent Door Midway Station in Adrian. The exact position of Route 66's "midway" point (equidistant from both Chicago and Los Angeles) is a matter of some dispute.

109

The Midpoint Café

Below: The interior of Adrian's Midpoint Café, the "official" halfway point of Route 66. The eatery is popular with both tourists and local residents.

The signs in its windows and by the road outside proclaim the Midpoint Café in Adrian to be precisely 1139 miles (1834km) from both Chicago and Los Angeles. It has been in business (under different names) since the 1920s, and has the distinction of being the oldest continuously run café anywhere on Route 66 in Texas, Oklahoma, or New Mexico. It started out as a single-room establishment with a dirt floor, owned by a local businesswoman, Jeannie VanderWort, and operated by Zella Prin as Zella's Café. After changing hands several times, it was redeveloped by Jessie Fincher

Above: A "halfway" sign opposite the Midpoint Café. Although Adrian is the approximate midway point, definitive mileages are impossible to calculate.

and Dub Edmond (who still lives nearby) and renamed Jessie's Café, before passing to its present proprietor, New Englander Fran Houser, in 1991. The Midpoint's walls are covered in photographs

chronicling its history, and in 1997, Fran opened a gift and antique shop on the premises. As she explained in an interview with Rick Storm of the *Amarillo Globe-News*, "We depend on our Route 66 customers, and in the winter, business goes to almost nil. We needed something to supplement the restaurant, and so far, I'm astounded at the support we've had."

The display of antiques, curios, and memorabilia gives visitors plenty to feast their eyes on while

Below: Outside the Midpoint Café. This photo was taken during the winter months, a quiet period for Route 66 tourism. In summer, the car park would be crammed with visitors' vehicles .

Below: Another more makeshift "midway" mileage post in Adrian.

waiting for Fran to serve up their choice of food; the café's menu includes "the best hamburger on Route 66," as well as freshly baked bread, pastries, and pies. She is proud of the Midpoint's landmark status among travelers, but equally appreciative of the backing she receives from Adrian's townspeople: "When our local customers come in and see that we're behind [with the service], they'll get up and pour some coffee and pitch in. This is a close community, and this café is one of the focal points after the school and church."

Right: Entering Glenrio – today, the "business spur" signposted here leads only to a ghost town.

Below: The derelict building near this sign, now surrounded by junk, was once the last (or first depending on the direction you are traveling) motel and café on Route 66 in Texas. It is seen here from the eastern side of Glenrio; the state line lies a few yards ahead.

West of Adrian, 66 comes to a dead end; we must join I-40 at exit 18 to complete our journey to the border town of Glenrio. In pre-Interstate days, driving conditions in this region, still sometimes difficult when the weather closes in, could demand remarkable levels of resourcefulness and cooperation from travelers. Former Greyhound bus driver Howard Suttle's book *Behind The Wheel* tells the story of how, after a jack-knifed truck had blocked the road near here, he and other road users joined forces to dig each other out of a snowdrift. "There were about ten or twelve truckers and motorists shoveling snow from around the rig, and some were bringing sand and spreading it by hand. In these cases, it is common courtesy to help if you can, to get the first one in line out of the way, the second and so on – until your turn comes around."

| 1113 | Bushland | 1125 | Vega | 1152 | Glenrio | 1180 | Bard | 1194 |
| Cadillac Ranch | 1116 | Wildorado | 1138 | Adrian | 1175 | Endee | 1189 | San Jon |

Left: Looking west from a bridge over the Interstate near Exit 0 at Glenrio.

Below: These cacti are among the few roadside plants that flourish in the arid conditions here.

Right: Looking back east toward the ruined motel and sign from the New Mexico side of Glenrio.

Before getting stuck near Adrian, Suttle, who was traveling east to Amarillo, had passed through Glenrio, which he describes as "a small village." This little border settlement – used as a location for John Ford's 1940 movie version of *The Grapes of Wrath*, starring Henry Fonda as Tom Joad – was once a significant staging post on 66. Part of it lies in Texas' Deaf Smith County (named for Erastus Smith (1787–1837), a scout in the Revolution against Mexican rule that took place during 1835–36). However, its western quarter is in Quay County, New Mexico, where lower taxes on gas and a more liberal attitude to alcohol led to a concentration of service stations and bars. Today, these have all vanished: and since the decommissioning of the Old Road and the construction of I-40, which passes just to the north, Glenrio has been almost utterly abandoned.

" **Where the trucks stop, that's where the customers come. Can't fool truck drivers, they know. They bring the custom. They know. Give 'em a stale cup a coffee an' they're off the joint. Treat 'em right an' they come back.** "

from The Grapes Of Wrath *by John Steinbeck, 1939*

New Mexico

66's path through New Mexico changed radically in the late 1930s, when its original alignment via Santa Fe was replaced by a new cutoff shortening the journey to Albuquerque by more than 80 miles (129km). This route is now followed by I-40, which has swallowed up much of the Old Road east of "Duke City." Beyond it, we pass through Indian lands on our journey toward the Continental Divide and the border.

*Above: Twilight at the 66 Diner, 1405 Central Avenue, Albuquerque.
This popular eatery, built inside the shell of a 1940s Phillips gas station,
is one of the attractions on the path of Route 66 through "Duke City."
Main picture: The remains of an old trading post a few yards west of
the Texas/New Mexico state line.*

New Mexico

Below: Major oil companies were keen to promote a picturesque image of America's highways, and produced many sponsored roadmaps like this one.

Several decades before New Mexico became a part of the USA in 1848, traders and travelers were entering the area from the east on the Santa Fe Trail, which stretched some 780 miles (1255km) from Missouri, via Kansas, Texas, and Colorado. The first railroad to serve the region, the Atchison, Topeka & Santa Fe, reached the Raton Pass (on the Colorado-New Mexico border) in 1878; soon afterwards, the line was extended to Santa Fe and Albuquerque.

In 1912, New Mexico was made a state, with Santa Fe as its capital; and in the following decade Cyrus Avery's committee chose to route their new highway through the mountain city, even though this involved a substantial detour from the road's regular east-west path. The earliest alignment of 66 turned north about 18 miles (29km) beyond Santa Rosa, reached Las Vegas, and

followed the path of the old trail to Santa Fe. It then headed south via Albuquerque to Los Lunas before looping back and continuing west towards Mesita (see pages 122-125 and 130-131).

After the opening of Route 66 in 1926, this meandering thoroughfare quickly attracted criticism from State Governor A.T. Hannett. As Sue Bohannan Mann explains in *Route 66 Magazine*, the Governor gave orders for the immediate construction of a more direct east-west cutoff that "would connect the road seven miles west of Santa Rosa to an existing highway." Hannett's dirt-surfaced road, which shortened the journey from Santa Rosa to Albuquerque by some 80 miles

Right: The famous Clines Corners reststop.

Below: The Fat Man guarantees "good eats" at Joseph's in Santa Rosa.

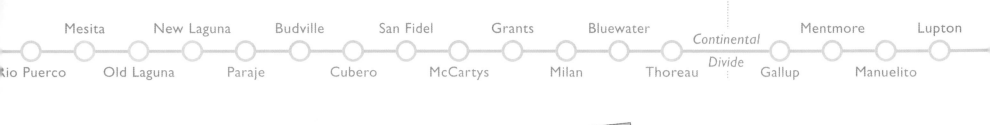
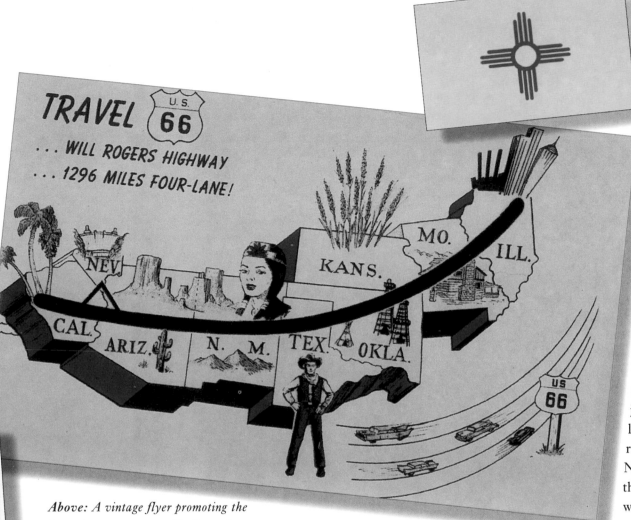

Above: A vintage flyer promoting the latest improvements to 66. Extra lanes were badly needed as traffic increased.

Below: On the road to nowhere – the last few yards of Route 66's southern frontage east of Tucumcari.

(129km), was completed, using "a motley collection of surplus World War I Caterpillars, tractors and graders", in early 1927. Its path was similar to that of the paved alignment that formally replaced the Santa Fe loop ten years later, when concreting on nearly all New Mexico's 395 miles (636km) of Route 66 had been completed.

Only about 110 miles (177km) of the Old Road are still driveable today, and the 69-mile (111km) stretch of I-40 between Santa Rosa and Moriarty is the longest unavoidable section of freeway we will encounter anywhere on our journey. However, the spectacular southwestern landscape and the rich heritage and culture of this region (which has been occupied and cultivated by Native Americans for some 10,000 years) ensure that traveling through the "Land of Enchantment" will be an unforgettable experience.

Below: The highway near San Jon seen from 66's southern frontage.

117

Below and beneath: San Jon's Old Route 66 Garage – still thriving, despite the coming of I-40, which has diverted traffic and business away from the center of town. The Old Road here is almost deserted as it sweeps west across the plains toward Tucumcari.

A few yards from the derelict sign for the first (or last) motel in Texas, we cross into New Mexico, and enter the Mountain Time Zone. Watches should be set back an hour – although there are no roadside reminders to do so until we reach Tucumcari, about 45 miles (72km) to the west.

The Old Road's original alignment led from Glenrio through Endee and Bard, which were notorious for their lawlessness during the Wild West era, but saw an influx of new residents after the establishment of Route 66 - many of them migrants from the Dustbowl who chose to settle here when they could afford to travel no longer. It is still possible to reach these two tiny settlements via a gravel-covered section of highway between Glenrio and the eastern edge of San Jon. This, though, can be hazardous in bad weather, and travelers wishing to avoid it should stay on I-40.

After reaching San Jon via the Interstate, exit onto the well-surfaced alignment of 66 that runs as a frontage alongside it. To the left, the Caprock, a ridge of rock stretching back into Texas, dominates the landscape. In the cliffs south of San Jon is the 1,000-seat Caprock Amphitheater; beyond it, about 80 miles (129km) southeast of Tucumcari, is Clovis, where Buddy Holly (1939-1959) recorded *Peggy Sue* and many of his other classic songs at studios run by producer Norman Petty.

Tucumcari itself is a significant regional centre, sited at the intersection of I-40 and US 54, the highway that leads northeast across the edges of Texas and Oklahoma en route to Kansas, Missouri and Illinois. In the old days, the city was a popular nightstop for users of the Old Road, and on 815 East Tucumcari Boulevard, its most celebrated motel, the Blue Swallow (which is featured in detail overleaf), is still open for business.

Right: Over the border: the first New Mexico Route 66 sign, at the roadside west of Glenrio.

1335	Moriarty	1366	Barton	1381	Albuquerque		Nine Mile Hill	1417
Clines Corners	1355	Edgewood	1369	Tijeras	1396	Rio Grande	1405	Rio Puerco

> " The radio gave out soon after she passed a faded sign that said, WELCOME TO NEW MEXICO! LAND OF ENCHANTMENT! It helped that almost immediately the flat-topped buttes of west Texas spread their wings, kind of, and became mountains. Enchantment, indeed. "
>
> *from* Rest Stop *by Lillian M. Roberts, 1999*

Above: *This eye-catching sign promotes Tucumcari's two biggest attractions: Native American goods and Route 66.*

Below: *Teepee Curios, on the path of Route 66 in downtown Tucumcari, is a long-standing favorite with tourists.*

Above: *Looking west on the southern frontage near Tucumcari. In this area, the "staked plains," through which the road has passed for hundreds of miles, are gradually giving way to a more undulating, rockier landscape.*

Blue Swallow Motel

Below, right and far right: Tucumcari's Blue Swallow, with its distinctive neon sign, is almost certainly the Old Road's longest-established motel. Opened in 1942, it was managed by Mrs. Lillian Redman for over 40 years. Since her death in 1999, it has been lovingly restored by its current owners.

The Blue Swallow, at 815 East Tucumcari Boulevard, is believed to be the oldest continuously operating motel anywhere on Route 66. Work started on its construction in 1939, and by 1942 it was open for business with 13 tourist cabins; the garages were added in 1948. Sixteen years later, the Blue Swallow was bought by a local trailer park owner, Floyd Redman, as an engagement present for his fiancée, Lillian (1909–1999). The future Mrs. Redman was a Texan

who had come west in 1916, and had worked as a "Harvey girl" (see pages 150-153) before her marriage. She proved to be the ideal proprietress for the Blue Swallow: over the next four decades the motel became famous for the homespun warmth of its welcome, and for Lillian's special rapport with the guests. She greeted each of them with a card expressing the hope "that you will be as comfortable and happy as if you were in your own home," and (as the motel had no internal phones) provided a personal morning wake-up service by knocking on their doors.

The Blue Swallow's reputation spread far and wide: the *Smithsonian* magazine described it as "the last, best and friendliest of the old-time motels." However, by 1998 Lillian Redman's health was failing, and the building, which had been listed on the National Register of Historic Places in 1993, was in need of repairs. Shortly before her death in 1999, Lillian sold it to a couple from Virginia, Gene and Shirley Shelton. It has since been taken over by new owners, Dale and Hilda Bakke, who have restored its famous neon sign to its former glory, installed authentic pre-war Western Electric phones in each room, and carried out other improvements. However, they are pledged to preserve the Blue Swallow's unique atmosphere and décor.

Below: The Blue Swallow is one of the Route 66 landmarks featured in a limited edition series of models by the Cat's Meow Village of Wooster, Ohio.

Right and below: The "Fat Man," created to promote the Club Café in Santa Rosa, now graces the façade of Joseph's on the city's Will Rogers Drive. His biscuits are still the best!

CLUB CAFE
ORIGINAL
ROUTE 66
SANTA ROSA, NM
Two Million Sourdough Biscuits
SINCE 1935

Far right and above far right: Cattle beside the southern frontage of Route 66 outside Palomas. I-40, which lies to the right of the picture, carries frequent billboards advertising Tucumcari as a stopover for long-distance travelers. The one shown here is visible only to eastbound traffic on the freeway.

Tucumcari began as a makeshift camp for railroad workers in the 1900s, and as late as 1922, one resident (quoted in Susan Croce Kelly's *Route 66*) recalled that its sole surfaced road "was paved with clinkers and cinders from the coal plant." However, the influx of travellers brought by Route 66 led to a steady improvement in the town's amenities; and by the 1940s, Tucumcari was offering visitors not just a bed for the night, but food, shopping and a range of other attractions. It has retained its appeal despite the decommissioning of the highway, and the striking "66" sculpture on Tucumcari Boulevard, created in 1997 by Thomas

Coffin, reflects the Old Road's enduring importance to the area.

On the next stage of our journey, we spend more time than usual away from Route 66, which disappears completely for 8 miles (13km) west of Tucumcari. After this enforced stretch on I-40, take the Palomas exit (321) to follow 66's original path to Montoya, Newkirk and Cuervo, before rejoining the Interstate at exit 291 for the remaining 18 miles (29km) to Santa Rosa. We enter the city on Will Rogers Drive, site of Joseph's Cantina, from whose frontage the famous "Fat Man" beams out at hungry travelers. The Fat

1335	Moriarty	1366	Barton	1381	Albuquerque		Nine Mile Hill	1417
Clines Corners	1355	Edgewood	1369	Tijeras	1396	Rio Grande	1405	Rio Puerco

CLINES CORNERS

Roy Cline, a native of Arkansas, migrated to New Mexico in the mid-1920s and tried his hand at a variety of enterprises there – managing a post office and a hotel before opening a service station at Lucy, a little settlement on the Santa Fe railroad. These all proved unsuccessful, and after some further upheavals, including a spell as a farmer back in Arkansas, Cline returned to New Mexico, purchased a parcel of land near the junction of Route 6 and Route 2 (later designated 66 and 285), and set up a roadside café and garage there. On more than one occasion, he was obliged to move when the highways themselves were realigned, but by the end of the decade, "Clines Corners" had established itself as a popular reststop, offering refreshments and gas to travelers on both roads. It was also a staging post for the Greyhound bus routes running through the region, and now attracts much of its business from Interstate users.

Above: A Clines Corners billboard beside I-40. This celebrated site has been serving travelers for over 70 years, and ads like the one shown here are dotted along the roadside for many miles to the east and west.

Man was formerly associated with the nearby Club Café, but since its closure, he has found a new home at Joseph's, whose owners, the Campos family, have acquired the rights to the logo.

Beyond Santa Rosa, 66 vanishes again until we reach the outskirts of Moriarty, about 75 miles (120km) to the west. Continuing on the Interstate towards Clines Corners, we pass the junction with US 84 where 66 originally turned off north towards Santa Fe; its later alignment, which we now follow to Albuquerque, dates from 1937.

Below: Conservation groups like the Native Plant Society of New Mexico play an active role in protecting the roadside and desert flora of this region.

The highway from Santa Rosa leads through the foothills of the Rockies. Mesas and mountains can be seen on either side of the road, although the Sangre de Christo range, with its peaks of up to 13,000 feet (3960m), lies well to the north. The Interstate does not follow the contours of this terrain as closely as 66 once did, but it continues to climb steadily; the town of Moriarty, about 20 miles (32km) west of Clines Corners, is over 6000 feet (1830m) above sea level. Here, we leave I-40 and join SR 333, which passes through Edgewood, reaches its highest elevation just west of Barton, and then begins a dramatic descent through Tijeras Canyon toward Albuquerque.

The city, founded in 1706, was named after Francisco Fernandez de la Cueva, Duke of Alburquerque (*sic*), and viceroy of New Spain. The modern spelling of "Albuquerque" was adopted after America gained control of the region in the Mexican War of 1846-48. Once a key staging post on El Camino Reál (the historic route between Santa Fe and Mexico City), "Duke City" owes much of its more recent prosperity to Route 66, which forms its "Main Street", Central Avenue.

Below: A strange sight by the side of SR333 (Route 66) near Barton. This mobile jail contains two dummy prisoners – including a distinctly undersized "Billy the Kid!"

Follow the signs into town, and then glance back at the mountains that tower to the east, revealing the extent of the 2,000 foot (610m) drop we have just made into the Rio Grande Valley. 66's pre-1937 alignment, coming from Las Vegas and Santa Fe, also had its share of impressive gradients. The postcard opposite shows the road winding down La Bajada Hill, about 35 miles (56km) northeast of here; having reached Albuquerque, it continued south to Los Lunas before finally turning west again. I-25 runs fairly close to this early alignment, and some stretches of the original 66 still survive nearby.

Right: Approaching Albuquerque on SR333. The road descends over 2000 feet (610m) as it heads west through Tijeras Canyon.

Above: Albuquerque by moonlight – looking east toward the Sandia Mountains towering above the city.

Right and far right: The steep gradients on the original alignments of the Old Road in this area provided a severe test for drivers and their vehicles.

LA BAJADA HILL, BETWEEN SANTA FE AND ALBUQUERQUE, NEW MEXICO

121023

Barton	1381	Albuquerque		Nine Mile Hill	1417	Mesita	1446	New Lag
1369	Tijeras	1396	Rio Grande	1405	Rio Puerco	1441	Old Laguna	144

Below: Albuquerque in the old days. A vintage postcard showing the city's downtown area, and photos of two popular hotels – the White Way Court, and the magnificent Alvarado, built adjacent to the Santa Fe railroad terminus, and demolished in the 1960s.

CENTRAL AVENUE, LOOKING WEST, ALBUQUERQUE, N. M.

ON U.S. HIGHWAY 66
One-Half Mile West of Albuquerque, N. M.
"In the Center of the Better Tourist Courts"

H-2895 THE ALVARADO, FRED HARVEY HOTEL, ALBUQUERQUE, NEW MEXICO

Probably the best way to experience Albuquerque is to take a leisurely drive along Central, stopping to observe its many attractions more closely. We start on its eastern section (beyond the point where it is crossed by I-25) and continue westward. At 1405 NE is the 66 Diner, an ingenious recreation of a "traditional" roadside restaurant, built within the shell of a 1940s Phillips gas station. Inside, the décor is pink and turquoise, and the 66's food, milk shakes, and juke box ("as badass as the chicken fried steak" according to its publicity) are all highly impressive.

West of I-25 and the railroad tracks, we come to the intersection with 2nd Street, where the side of a mortgage finance office is the surprising location for "The Mother Road" – Joe Stephenson's striking mural devoted to Route 66, and unveiled in 1995. Albuquerque is a rich location for public art, but the architectural jewel in its crown is undoubtedly the KiMo Theatre on Central and 5th. This "Pueblo Deco"-style picture palace was designed by the Boller brothers, who specialized in exotic buildings, and imbued the KiMo (whose name comes from an Amerindian word for "mountain lion" or "king of its kind") with many distinctively southwestern and Native American features. Opened in 1927, it once housed a restaurant and a radio station as well as its stage and screen. After a severe fire and a period of decline in the 1960s, the KiMo was purchased by the city of Albuquerque in 1977, and has now been fully restored.

Continuing west along Central, the main downtown area gives way to the Old Town district, and we soon reach the river. Route 66 crosses the Rio Grande on the Old Town Bridge, and begins the long climb out of the city via Nine Mile Hill.

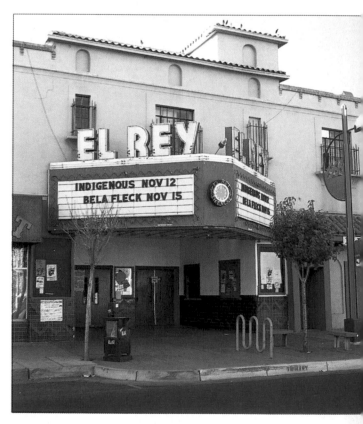

Above: The El Rey lies a little west of the Ki-Mo, at 620 NW Central. Originally built as a cinema, it presents a wide range of live concerts by leading rock, blues, and world music performers.

Left: The Ki-Mo Theater, downtown on Albuquerque's Central and Fifth. This Pueblo Deco-style venue dates from 1927, and was undergoing restoration when this photograph was taken. It has since reopened to the general public.

Below: Central Avenue boasts a proliferation of stores, eateries, and bars. Many of these roadside businesses date back to the heyday of Route 66.

· VOICE OF THE ROAD ·

Jack D. Rittenhouse

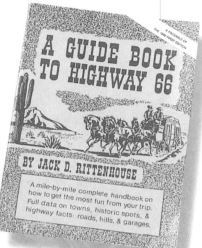

Jack D. Rittenhouse (1912–1991), a longtime resident of Albuquerque, was the first man to compile a detailed guide to the Old Road. He had the idea of writing a handbook for travelers on Route 66 during the War years, when, as he explained in 1988, "I realized that there might be a great postwar migration from the eastern states to California.[...] I knew that most easterners had serious worries about crossing the mountains and deserts. I had made several runs over the route, so I dug into the research needed to do a proper guidebook. Then in March 1946 I made a last, careful round trip to double-check my facts.

"That trip was made in a 1939 American Bantam coupé...To inspect the scenery...I drove from dawn to dusk at 35 miles an hour. There were no tape recorders then, so I scrawled notes on a big yellow pad on the seat beside me. Each night I dug out my portable manual typewriter and typed my notes." The result of Rittenhouse's labors, his famous Guide Book to Highway 66, appeared in 1946, and was reissued in a facsimile edition by the University of New Mexico Press two years before his death.

Right: Pearl's Dive Bar & Grill on Central – its huge illuminated "bottle-top" sign is even more garish at night!

127

Public art

Opposite page, above: "The Mother Road/El Camino de los Caminos" – mural at Central and 2nd, Albuquerque, NM, designed by Joe Stephenson for Working Classroom Inc. (co-sponsored by New Mexico Finance Authority).
Opposite page, below: Trompe l'oeil mural by "Fox," 4th Street, Sayre, OK.
Below: "McLean, The Heart of Old Route 66" mural at the junction of 1st Street (Route 66) and Rowe, McLean, TX.

Much of the art on Route 66 celebrates the heritage of the highway and the places it passes through. Sometimes, the work on display is directly commemorative – like the statue of "Bunion Derby" winner Andy Payne in Foyil, Oklahoma – but often it has a subtler, more interactive relationship with its surroundings. *Trompe l'oeil* murals, like those in Quapaw and Sayre, Oklahoma, help to recapture the time when the main drags of these little towns were throbbing arteries of America's Main Street, alive with travelers and traders. Further west, artwork expands in scale and scope to reflect the immensity of the landscape; one piece on display near Albuquerque interweaves past and present by showing cars and trucks sharing the highway with wagon trains.

New Mexico has been particularly active in nurturing public art through a variety of state-sponsored and locally run schemes. In the early 1990s, the recognition that "for centuries, murals have been an important public art forum to Native American and Hispanic cultures" led Albuquerque city officials to implement a Murals Program,

encouraging contributions from a wide range of professional, apprentice and amateur artists. This project has resulted in the creation of works such as "The Mother Road" on Central and 2nd – one of a series of downtown murals produced in association with Working Classroom (an organization providing training and support for talented young minority artists) and co-sponsored by local businesses.

Meanwhile, in Winslow, Arizona, direct contributions from members of the public (who can purchase bricks engraved with names or messages) have helped to fund a remarkable site that draws its inspiration from the classic Eagles song *Take It Easy*. "On the Corner," appropriately located on the town's Second and Kinsley, combines the work of Nevada-based sculptor Ron Adamson and Californian muralist John Pugh; it was unveiled in 1999.

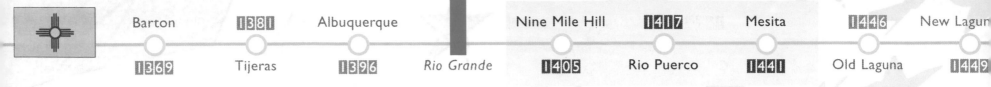
Below: The Parker Truss road bridge at Rio Puerco, built in 1933, is now closed to traffic, but was once a vital Route 66 river crossing. Note the yellow warning sign; the structure was unable to accommodate vehicles taller than 13ft 8in (approx. 4m).

As 66 climbs to the top of Nine Mile Hill, which lies exactly 9 miles (14km) from downtown Albuquerque, there are splendid views of the city and the Sandia mountains to the east. At the top of the hill is a junction with I-40 (exit 149); to stay on 66, cross the freeway and head west on the northern frontage road. Nearby is the Rio Puerco, whose tendency to flooding once posed severe problems for Route 66's roadbuilders. An earlier crossing a few miles downstream was swept away in 1929, and four years later this was replaced by the Parker Truss-type bridge that still stands here (see pages 40-41 for more details of this design). Constructed from ten 25-foot (7.6m) panels, it is the longest single-span model of its type in New Mexico.

At this point, there is another unavoidable stretch of I-40 in prospect: join the Interstate again at exit 140 and continue until exit 117 for Mesita. On the way there, we pass the junction with NM 6 (exit 126); this was where Route 66's old, pre-1937 alignment (see pages 122-125) reconnected with the more modern highway after its detour south via Los Lunas.

The road now approaches Indian lands - long-established pueblos (the word is Spanish for 'village') occupied by the Laguna and Acoma Native American communities, who speak the same Keresan language, and have their own governors, religious and social practices and culture. Mesita

Left: Roadside billboard for the Oasis Café, on the north side of Route 66 not far from the summit of Nine Mile Hill.

Below and right: The long ascent of Nine Mile Hill – looking back east toward Albuquerque.

1452 · Paraje · Budville · 1455 · 1457 · Cubero · San Fidel · 1461 · 1466 · McCartys · Grants · 1477 · 1483 · Milan · Bluewater · 1491 · 1510 · Thoreau

itself is an outlying part of Old Laguna, and the highway between the two settlements leads through a landscape of mesas, buttes and boulders. As Bob Moore and Patrick Grauwels observe in their *Illustrated Guidebook* to Route 66, it is sobering to think that this was once a major thoroughfare, used daily by hundreds of cars, trucks and buses.

Right: The Rio Grande Valley, seen through the morning haze and the dust stirred up by wind and traffic on Nine Mile Hill.

Above: Beyond exit 117 on I-40, Old Route 66 snakes away toward the Native American pueblo at Mesita.

131

Old Laguna is the capital of the Laguna pueblo. It was established in its present form in 1699, when its Mission Church, St. Joseph's, was built by Franciscan friars from stone and adobe, but is also the site of a previous Native American settlement dating back to the 14th century. Today, the pueblo comprises six villages – Laguna itself, Mesita, Paraje, Paguate, Encinal, and Seama – and has a total population of about 8000. Visitors should note that the pueblo lands are occasionally closed to the public, and that there are also some restrictions on photography, which is not permitted inside the Mission Church itself.

The highway – still "Old 66" although it is classified SR 124 – now heads towards New Laguna and Paraje (whose name is Spanish for "stopping place"). Here, a backroad leads south to the region's other major pueblo at Acoma – suggesting a side trip that may attract many travelers keen to see the

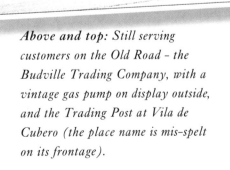

Above and top: Still serving customers on the Old Road - the Budville Trading Company, with a vintage gas pump on display outside, and the Trading Post at Vila de Cubero (the place name is mis-spelt on its frontage).

Right: The Trading Company building at Paraje, just east of Budville.

Left: The Paraje Trading Company's fading paintwork still stands out amid the rocks and scrub of the surrounding landscape.

ancient mesa-top "city in the sky." Road historian Jack D. Rittenhouse, who took the detour, commented that "a visit to this remarkable place is practically a 'must'."

66 itself continues west: about 3 miles (5km) from Paraje lies Budville, a small settlement named for H.N. "Bud" Rice, proprietor of an automobile service business which he opened in 1928 and ran from the Budville Trading Post. In November 1967, Bud's son (also called Bud) and a elderly woman were shot dead at the Trading Post during a hold-up; two arrests were subsequently made, but no one was ever convicted of the crimes.

Next, we come to Cubero; novelist Ernest Hemingway (1899–1961) stayed near here while writing *The Old Man and the Sea* (1952). To the north, Mount Taylor towers above the landscape, while SR 124 leads through the once-busy trading center of San Fidel before approaching a junction with I-40.

Above and inset: St. Joseph's Church, constructed from stone and adobe, lies at the heart of the Old Laguna pueblo. Dating from the 17th century (but built on a much older site) it is still the main place of worship for its surrounding community.

Harley-Davidson FL

ROUTE 66

The FL 74 Knucklehead shown here is finished in "flight red." These motorcycles were also available in clipper blue, cruiser green, black or (for export models) olive green, although color choice was restricted after the outbreak of war.

Right: Shell supplied gas to the Soulsby Station at Mount Olive, IL, probably the oldest outlet on 66.

The history of the motorcycle manufacturing firm founded in 1903 by William Harley and the Davidson brothers of Milwaukee is one of innovations, broken records – in 1921, a Harley was the first-ever bike to win a race at average speed of over 100mph (161kph) – and business acumen. Like

SHELL GASOLINE

The upgraded 16-inch tires on the new 74 provided a smoother ride, whatever the road surface encountered by the machine.

Stainless steel trim strips decorate the gas tank. This Deluxe model 74 also boasts a chromed instrument panel and rims.

The 74 has a steel, double downtube frame, spring-fork suspension, and weighs in at a hefty 575lb (261kg).

other manufacturers, Harley suffered a severe sales slump during the Depression, but it recovered quickly, continuing to develop new machines while its rivals struggled to stay in business. And in the year of America's entry into World War II (during which it was a major supplier of bikes to the military) it produced this update to its already-powerful Knucklehead model, boosting the engine size to 74 inches (1200cc) to create one of the biggest, most formidable machines on the road.

This FL is owned by Armando Magri of Sacramento, California.

The 45° V-twin engine gave the 74 a maximum speed of 95mph (153kph).

Right: The remains of the Whiting Bros. gas station at McCartys; when this was destroyed by fire, part of an older roadside business was found inside.

Below: The "Malpais" (badlands) on the road to Grants, shot from exit 89 on I-40 (the junction of SR117 with the Interstate). The black, volcanic rocks seen in the foreground are a distinctive feature of this desolate, barren terrain.

Far right: The Roarin' 20's roadhouse in Grants is sited on Santa Fe Avenue (Route 66), the town's main drag.

At exit 96 on I-40 near McCartys, Route 66 (SR 124) crosses from the north to the south side of the freeway. Here stand the fire-damaged ruins of a Whiting Bros. gas station (see pages 102–103 for more details about the company), built on the site of an older roadside diner and store, the Chef's Rancho Café. After the construction of the Whiting Bros. station, the Rancho was hidden inside the new building – until the fire burned away the walls to reveal part of the original structure, as shown in the photographs on this page.

About five miles (8km) beyond McCartys, the road returns (through a tunnel) to the northern frontage of I-40; at exit 89, take SR 117, which leads towards the town of Grants, passing through the so-called Malpais or "badlands." This ancient volcanic area, strewn with beds of black lava, was described by Jack D. Rittenhouse as a place of "deserted pueblos, rumored hidden treasure…veins of ore, and the hideouts of early bandits." Approximately 25 miles (40km) to the south is the Bandera Ice Cave, a frozen pocket of water trapped within the lava after an ancient volcanic eruption, whose ice remains perpetually below zero whatever the outside

> ❝ In the United States there is more space where nobody is than where anybody is. That is what makes America what it is. ❞
>
> *from* The Geographical History of America
> *by Gertrude Stein, 1936*

temperature. The cave is privately owned, but guided tours are available, and another nearby landmark well worth a visit is the famous sandstone cliff known as "Inscription Rock" (El Morro). This is located in the Ramah Navajo Reservation, and is covered in carved signatures and other markings.

Grants, the first fairly sizeable town on the highway west of Albuquerque, began as a railroad camp (the Santa Fe line to Los Angeles still passes through it) and later became a popular overnight stop for drivers on 66. The Old Road heads down the town's Santa Fe Avenue before crossing the railroad tracks, and continuing towards Milan on SR 122.

Right: These signs for the defunct Whiting Bros. gas station and its associated businesses still stand near I-40 and SR 124.

Right: The El Rancho offers a taste of old-style luxury, and has recently started to provide motel accommodation for its guests.

Above: Gallup, the last sizeable town on 66 in New Mexico, is a major center for Native American art, and also a popular location for moviemakers.

Milan, just west of Grants, is a comparatively new community, built in the mid-1950s and named for Salvador Milan, owner of the land on which it stands; the small settlement of Bluewater lies about eight miles (13km) to its west. Route 66, running just north of the Interstate, is now surrounded by mesas, with the Cibolla National Forest and the Zuni Mountains visible on its southern side. We have been climbing fairly steadily since leaving the Rio Grande Valley over 90 miles (145km) earlier. The town of Thoreau, which we pass through next, is 7200 feet above sea level; and five miles (8km) farther on, the highway approaches North America's Continental Divide. To the east of here, water flows east to the Atlantic Ocean; to the west, it empties into the Pacific: and, at 7275 feet (2217m), the Divide is one of the highest-lying places on the length of the Old Road.

Right: The El Rancho Hotel on the path of Route 66 in downtown Gallup - a filmstars' favorite since the 1930s, now restored to its former glory.

CONTINENTAL DIVIDE
ELEVATION
7,275 ft
RAINFALL DIVIDES AT THIS POINT.
WEST DRAINS INTO THE PACIFIC...
EAST DRAINS INTO THE ATLANTIC.

Beyond the Continental Divide, we rejoin I-40 for the journey toward Gallup, leaving the freeway again at exit 36. The city, known as "The Indian Capital of the USA", is renowned as a center for Native American art and jewellery, but also boasts a more diverse artistic and architectural heritage. Its notable buildings include the recently restored El Rancho Hotel, which dates from 1937, and was popular with Hollywood greats such as Spencer Tracy, Katharine Hepburn, and Kirk Douglas; and the El Morro Theater on Coal Avenue, designed by the Boller brothers and opened in 1928.

West of the town, we reach the last few miles of Route 66 in New Mexico. SR 118 leads through Mentmore, Manuelito (named for the Navajo chief who opposed the forced removal of his people from their native lands in the 1860s), and towards Lupton, just across the state line.

Above and inset above: The Continental Divide, west of Thoreau, should be an exciting location - but seems dull and uncultivated in comparison to the vivid colors of the vintage postcard also shown here.

Arizona

Despite its dry climate, Arizona's name is derived from an Indian word for "little spring." However, the state includes not only desert and what John Steinbeck called "sun-rotted mountains," but the refreshing climate of Flagstaff - a city which 66 helped to establish as a tourist attraction. Further west, an uninterrupted section of the Old Road leads via Truxton and Kingman to the steep gradients of the Sitgreaves Pass.

*Above: A stark reminder of the hazards awaiting travelers on the desert stretches of 66. In older vehicles with no air conditioning, ice and water were essentials. **Main picture:** The Route 66 Visitor Center in Hackberry – a treasure trove of Old Road artifacts.*

Arizona

Below: A saguaro cactus framed against the setting sun beside Route 66. The saguaro's blossom is Arizona's offical state flower.

The earliest Europeans to explore Arizona were 16th-century Spanish adventurers seeking gold, and the area was subsequently ruled by Mexico before passing to American control in 1848. Nine years later, the first wagon route through the territory was surveyed by Naval Lieutenant Edward Fitzgerald Beale (see pages 158-159).

The railroad arrived in the 1880s, when a Santa Fe subsidiary, the Atlantic and Pacific, began building its tracks west toward the Colorado River; many of the towns now on Route 66 grew up alongside the line. Soon, the Santa Fe was attracting tourists to Arizona, and providing them with luxurious accommodation in the "Harvey Houses" developed in association with British-born hotelier Fred Harvey (see pages 150-151); the first of these opened at the railroad station in Williams in 1908.

Highway travel in the region (which achieved statehood in 1912) was far less comfortable. According to one source, the roads between Phoenix and Los Angeles during this period were "unpaved trails across the desert vastness and rugged mountains…As recently as 1929, Arizona had less than 300 miles of paved highways." Route 66 was not completely concreted here until 1937, and working on the road was a harsh and demanding job. One contractor, Nathan James Skokusen, was responsible for overseeing construction between Williams and Seligman – a task that took nearly five years, using primitive machinery and teams of mules. In *Route 66 Magazine*, Skokusen's son, who occasionally stayed on site with his parents, described the conditions the engineers and laborers faced: "Dad set up work camps, complete with cook

Below: The Route 66 Visitor Center in Hackberry boasts a superb collection of roadside memorabilia – including the Burma Shave and Mobilgas "Flying Horse" signs shown here.

shacks. Workers had tents and cots…We lived in tents [too]. Mom spent much of her time stoking the wood/coal stove…Meals consisted of pinto beans, different meats [and] canned vegetables…highway officials would often be in the area just when it was chow time."

A large proportion of the 400 mile (644km) route through Arizona can still be driven on the Old Road, although two extensive stretches (between Chambers and Holbrook, and Winslow and Winona) have not survived. 66's original alignment via the Sitgreaves Pass and Oatman was bypassed in 1951, when a new, more direct highway from Kingman to Topock was introduced. Its path was later followed by I-40, which was built through the state from 1967 to 1984.

Above: Route 66 at Crookton Road, west of Ash Fork. I-40 is just visible to the left of the picture.

Left: In Arizona's Sacramento Valley, west of Kingman. Route 66 heads through this rocky landscape before beginning its winding ascent through the Sitgreaves Pass (visible to the right of the picture). West of here, the road climbs to a height of 3515 feet (1071m) above sea level.

The Freightliner Coronado tractor – a recent model designed specifically for independent truckers. Its 1500in^2 (9678cm^2) radiator provides cooling for its Class 8 diesel engine; units from 425 to 600hp are available.

ROUTE 66 Freightliner Coronado

Soundproofing and air conditioning make the Coronado comfortable to drive or sleep in.

The origins of Freightliner, which describes itself as "North America's Highway Truck Company," date back to the late 1930s, when Leland James, the proprietor of a freight transportation firm in Portland, Oregon, was seeking a manufacturer to build lightweight but powerful trucks to his specifications. No existing truck maker was interested, so James and a group of investors formed Freightliner Corporation to create the vehicles for themselves. Freightliner's aluminum, rust-resistant trucks could carry heavier payloads than rival rigs. Soon other firms were ordering them, and the Freightliner range grew rapidly; its many innovations have included all-aluminum sleepers, and the first cab capable of a 90° tilt. Since 1981 it has worked in partnership with DaimlerChrysler, the world leader in heavy-duty truck construction.

Above: "Snortin' Norton," drawn by Bill Boyd – the famous logo for the Campbell "66" Express Company of Springfield, MO.

Left: A fleet of trucks belonging to the Clinton Transfer & Storage Company of Blacksburg, VA; this photo probably dates from the early 1950s.

Right: Rigs like this were once commonplace on Route 66, where drivers often had to cope with hazardous road conditions – especially in poor weather.

Left: A steel-bodied tractor and trailer photographed on Route 66 in Texas in the 1960s.

The border settlement of Lupton, on the south frontage road off I-40's exit 359, is part of the vast surrounding Navajo Indian Reservation, and specializes in selling Native American goods and souvenirs to visitors via its Chief Yellowhorse Trading Post. Stay on the frontage road for a few more miles, then rejoin the freeway until exit 346; here, Route 66 heads north towards Querino Canyon via a stretch of unpaved highway. It eventually reconnects with I-40 at exit 342, east of Sanders – a tiny settlement that can be explored by turning off the freeway again, or bypassed by staying on the interstate.

Left Looking east down the unpaved Querino Canyon road – this rough surface makes for slow driving, and the passing miles may take their toll on your tires!

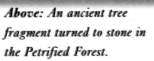
Above: An ancient tree fragment turned to stone in the Petrified Forest.

Right: The first major landmark on Route 66 in Arizona – the Yellowhorse Trading Post, near exit 359 on I-40, just inside the border.

1714	Winona	1742	Bellemont	1760	Williams	1796	Seligman	1855
Twin Arrows	1725	Flagstaff	1749	Parks	1777	Ash Fork	1826	Grand Canyon Caverns

Beyond Chambers, six miles (10km) from Sanders, we have another unavoidable spell on I-40, which leads past Navajo, and on toward the exit for the Petrified Forest National Park. The park lies within the larger Painted Desert region, where the rocks and sand making up the arid ground have oxidized at differing rates to create a kaleidoscope of sparkling colors. The Forest offers an even more extraordinary sight: here, the desert floor is littered with ancient, petrified tree stumps and logs, many of which appear astonishingly "wood-like" – though touching them confirms that they have indeed been turned to stone. A 28-mile (45km) scenic drive through the park provides excellent opportunities to examine and photograph the trees; there is also a Visitor Center and Museum; more details about it can be found on pages 188-189.

The journey west continues, via the Interstate, across the plains to Holbrook – an important staging post on the Old Road, and one of the first locations

> ## " The United States themselves are essentially the greatest poem. "
>
> *from* Leaves of Grass *by Walt Whitman , 1855*

Above and right: The extraordinary landscape of the Painted Desert and Petrified Forest, photographed on the scenic drive through this National Parkland.

to offer tourist camp accommodation for travelers. However, the most famous place to stay in town remains the Wigwam Village Motel on West Hopi Drive, whose concrete "tents" have been attracting overnight guests since 1950. The Wigwam Village is still run by the family of its founder, local resident Chester E. Lewis.

Above and below: Distinctive signs for the Jackrabbit Trading Post near Joseph City – a famous Old Road site dating from the 1940s, which still attracts thousands of visitors every year.

olbrook was founded in 1881, when the Atlantic and Pacific railroad built its tracks through a riverside settlement then known as Horsehead Crossing. The newly developed town that grew up nearby was named for Henry R. Holbrook, the Atlantic and Pacific's first Chief Engineer, and by all accounts, its early history was unsettled and frequently violent. However, by 1895, Holbrook was respectable enough to become the seat for the surrounding Navajo County; and three years later, its imposing courthouse was opened at the junction of Navajo and Arizona. This building (incorporating a jail) remained in use until 1976, and

Far right: Holbrook has always been a popular overnight stopping place for travelers on Route 66. This long-established motel, the Moen Kopi, is located downtown on the city's Kopi Drive.

now serves as a Museum. Holbrook's heritage as a Route 66 center is reflected in its colorful downtown diners, motels, and stores, and it remains a highly enjoyable place to visit.

Leave Holbrook via Hopi Drive, rejoin the interstate, and head for exit 274, about 13 miles (21km) out of town. Here, the frontage road leads towards the Jackrabbit Trading Post near Joseph City – one of the best-known, most effectively advertised businesses anywhere on Route 66. James

Left and above: Holbrook's Wigwam Motel – a perennially popular attraction on the city's West Hopi Drive. Opened in 1950 by local resident Chester E. Lewis, its concrete "tents" have recently been renovated.

Taylor, who opened the store in 1947, had a near-obsessive enthusiasm for publicity, and would regularly travel the highway in a truck, erecting his distinctive yellow Jackrabbit signs wherever he could. His shrewd tactics helped to establish the trading post's appeal for refreshment- and souvenir-hungry tourists, and today, under the proprietorship of Antonio and Cindy Jaquez, it remains as successful as ever.

West of the Trading Post, the frontage road reconnects with I-40 at exit 269. As we travel on the Interstate toward the turnoff for Winslow at exit 257, 17 miles (27km) away, the landscape near the road remains flat and featureless, but Humphreys Peak and the other mountains in the San Francisco range around Flagstaff are already becoming visible in the distance, surrounded by forests.

Above: One of the Jackrabbit Post's brightly decorated sidewalls. The building boasts a range of other Native American-style murals, as well as pictures of cacti and – inevitably – a plethora of black rabbit silhouettes.

149

Hotels and motels

Below: The rich colors of this old tinted postcard show off the stone-faced frontage, green roof and balcony, and apparently immaculate forecourt of the White Rock Court in Kingman, AZ.

By the late 19th century, the railroads had made comfortable long distance travel a reality, thanks to innovations like the sleeping car, designed in the 1860s by Chicago-based inventor George Mortimer Pullman (1831–1897) and soon widely adopted on long haul routes. The Santa Fe took passenger care a stage further in 1876, forming a partnership with Frederick Harvey (1835–1901), an Englishman whose company went on to launch a series of successful restaurants and hotels adjacent to the line's depots. These were staffed by the celebrated "Harvey Girls": smart, highly trained young women, recruited mostly from the eastern USA, who, as Will Rogers famously commented, "kept the West in food and wives." Many chose to marry and settle in the areas where they worked, and some, like Lillian Redman (see pages 120-121), subsequently became hoteliers themselves.

For early drivers, there was nothing to match the elegant amenities enjoyed by the rail customer. Few downtown inns had space for cars, and motorists pitching tents alongside the highway risked incurring the wrath of local farmers and landowners. It was not until the 1920s that cheap, basic accommodation for road travelers appeared, in the form of "motor camps:" open-air camping grounds with communal laundries and washrooms.

These spartan facilities were gradually superseded by sites providing individual huts containing beds; as many as 400,000 such "shacks for autoists" were built between 1929 and 1933. They, in turn, were the forerunners of the typical

Left and above top: The long-established Western Motel, still open for business on OKC's 39th Expressway.

Above right: A now vanished tourist court in Albuquerque, NM.

Above: Stagecoach 66 Motel, east of Seligman, AZ.
Top left: Du Bean's Motel Inn, Flagstaff, AZ.
Top right: An inn owned by the Whiting Bros. chain on the Kingman-Topock route now followed by I-40.

Right: This derelict motel, situated on the path of 66 at the Oklahoma/Texas border, lost its customers after the Old Road was bypassed.

"tourist court" – a semi-circular layout of cabins around a manager's office. Soon, most courts had running water in their rooms, and over the following years air conditioning, radio, and (eventually) TV were introduced. Their evolution into modern motel premises was completed when rooms, offices, and (sometimes) parking spaces were all brought together under the same roof in a single, contiguous structure.

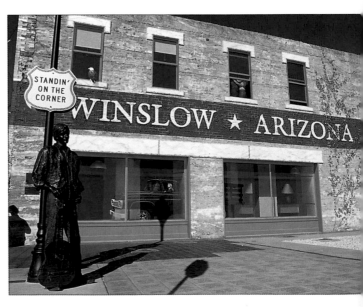

Below: Vivid images of downtown Winslow in the heyday of the Old Road. These rare postcards, dating from the 1930s and 1940s, are from the archives of Route 66 Magazine.

Like Holbrook, Winslow was originally a railroad town, settled during the westward expansion of the Atlantic and Pacific in the early 1880s. Named for a senior A & P official, it was incorporated in 1890, and subsequently became the site of the last and greatest of the station hotels created by the Fred Harvey Company in association with the Santa Fe, co-builder of the A & P line. The hotel, named La Posada, was designed by architect Mary Colter (1869–1958) in the style of an 18th century hacienda – with a tower, adobe walls, painted ceilings, and extensive gardens. There are two entrances: one facing the highway (East 2nd Street), the other by the railroad tracks. In its heyday, La Posada attracted distinguished guests such as Charles Lindbergh and Howard Hughes, but its fortunes declined in the postwar period, and it went out of business in 1957. However, it has now been acquired by a new owner, Allan Affeldt, who has restored and reopened it.

Winslow's other great claim to fame is, of course, its mention in Glenn Frey and Jackson Browne's song *Take It Easy*, featured on The Eagles' debut album in 1972. The "corner in Winslow, Arizona" referred to in its lyrics is celebrated by a sign at Kinsley and 2nd, and an adjacent "park" (appropriately named *On the Corner*) created by artists Ron Adamson and John Pugh (see pages 128–129), features a statue, engraved bricks and a mural.

After leaving town, we continue west on I-40. Little of the Old Road survives here, although we can turn off the Interstate to visit settlements like Meteor City (exit 239) and Twin Arrows (exit 219) before reaching Winona – aptly described in Tom Snyder's *Route 66 Traveler's Guide* as a "one-blink town," but immortalized by a line in Bobby Troup's *(Get Your Kicks On) Route 66* – "Flagstaff, Arizona, don't forget Winona…".

Left and inset: These giant wooden arrows, clearly visible from I-40, are a highly effective advertisement for the Twin Arrows Trading Post 11 miles (18km) east of Winona. The diner here serves classic American road food, and is especially popular with truckers.

Below: The residents of Meteor City, c.1950! Today, the little settlement boasts a store with a 60ft (18m) mural by Bob Waldmire, and a short fragment of the Old Road survives nearby.

Left: Railroad and landscape seen from the overpass at the Winona turnoff (exit 211) on I-40.

Far left: "Standin' on the Corner" at Kinsley and 2nd in Winslow – a statue by Ron Adamson, unveiled in 1999 to commemorate the classic Eagles song.

Right: Looking west toward the junction of Route 66 (running straight ahead) and San Francisco in Flagstaff's "Historic Downtown Railroad District." The railroad station is just out of shot to the left.

ENTERING
PRIVATE
LAND
15 M.P.H.

Above: The railroad depot at Williams. This train is one of several daily services carrying tourists north to the Grand Canyon. The two men in the foreground are part of a troupe of performers who provide entertainment before and during the journey.

At Winona, we leave the Interstate (exit 211) and turn right onto Camp Townsend/Winona Road; this eventually connects with US 89, which heads into Flagstaff. The city, lying nearly 7000 feet (2130m) above sea level, is said to have acquired its name following an incident in 1876, when scouts in the surrounding forests celebrated Independence Day by stripping a huge pine of its branches and flying an American flag from it. The landmark soon started to figure in directions for travelers, who were instructed to "Head straight west till you come to that flagstaff."

Route 66 runs through the heart of the city's "Historic Downtown Railroad District." This boasts a lovingly preserved 1925 train depot, as well as many attractive stores and restaurants. We rejoin the Interstate on the edge of town; after about seven miles (11km), a partially paved alignment near Bellemont (exit 185) offers a pleasant detour through Brannigan Park, climbing to the highest point on the Old Road (7387 feet/2250m), then dropping back to pass through Parks. The highway, shaded by tall ponderosa pines, continues towards Pittman Valley, where a left turn (beyond the on-ramp to the Interstate) leads to an alignment that skirts Davenport Lake before returning to I-40 at exit 167.

· VOICE OF THE ROAD ·

Paul Taylor

Paul Taylor, who lives with his wife Sandi in Williams, Arizona, is Publisher and Executive Editor of Route 66 Magazine, which provides news and information about what he calls "the most magical road in all the world." Paul grew up near Springfield, Illinois, traveling the highway with his parents on family vacations in the 1940s; after Navy service, he became an executive with a California-based advertising and public relations firm. Following his retirement, Paul began working as a freelance writer, and he and Sandi spent five years trailering the desert Southwest with their daughter Jessi. The couple launched Route 66 Magazine in 1993; as Paul explains, "when [its] premier issue hit the newsstands...phones started ringing and things really got busy." The quarterly magazine – and the Mother Road itself – soon became a major commitment for the Taylors, who also run a flourishing Route 66 gift shop in Williams. However, they still make time to travel the entire length of the highway at least three times a year.

Above left: An unpaved stretch of road near Brannigan Park, between Flagstaff and Williams. Despite the warning signs, this alignment is well worth exploring.

Left: Route 66 passing through downtown Williams. The headquarters of Paul and Sandi Taylor's Route 66 Magazine (displaying the flags and sign) is on the left, at number 326.

From here, it is only about four miles (6km) to the turnoff for Williams – founded in 1882, and named for "mountain man" Bill Williams (1787–1849), a scout and trapper who was one of the earliest white settlers in the area. Among the many attractions here are the depot for the Grand Canyon steam railroad line (dating from 1908), and the lovingly preserved town center, whose motels and stores date from 66's glory days. Williams holds a uniquely poignant position in the history of the highway: in 1984, it became the last place on the Old Road to be bypassed by the Interstate.

Below: The striking sign for the Stagecoach 66 Motel, east of Seligman Despite its name, the Stagecoach lies just off the path of the Old Road.

West of Williams, we rejoin I-40 for the 19-mile (30km) trip to Ash Fork – which lies just north of the Interstate, and can be reached from exit 146. The town, which takes its name from a clump of trees at a fork in the nearby Ash Creek, became the site of a railroad depot in 1882, but was destroyed by fire 11 years later, and subsequently rebuilt across the tracks from its original location. Its main industry is the quarrying and shipping of flagstones; several of its busy stoneyards are visible from the road.

About six miles (9km) out of Ash Fork, we come to the Crookton Road turnoff on I-40 (exit 139). At this point, we leave the Interstate and head northwest on a long, uninterrupted stretch of Route 66 that runs from here to Topock, on the Arizona/California border. Several old, abandoned alignments are visible on its first, 24-mile (39km) section, which passes just south of the 7160 ft (2182m) Trinity Mountain, and leads to Seligman, a town that grew up around a Santa Fe repair depot established in 1897.

In its earlier days, Seligman's residents used the railroad to overcome the area's chronic shortage of water; supplies were brought in on tank cars from the Chino Valley, 40 miles (64km) to the south, and sold to house-holders at 50¢ a barrel. Trains and roads also played a key role in establishing the town as an important center for livestock transportation. Today, it is the base for the Historic Route 66 Association of Arizona, founded in 1987 by local barber and long-time resident Angel Delgadillo, who remains its President Emeritus. Angel's brother Juan runs the popular Snow-Cap Drive In diner on Seligman's East Chino Street; nearby, on West Chino, is another well-known Route 66 eatery, the Copper Cart.

Above: A Confederate Flag flies outside the long-established Route 66 Grill in downtown Ash Fork.

Above: The Copper Cart Café, on Seligman's West Chino Street, offers customers what it describes as "Home Cooking on Historic Route 66" – including an all-day breakfast and a special ground beef and onion "sizzler."

Right: Despite a population of less than 600, Ash Fork is sometimes known as the "Flag Stone Capital of the United States." This busy stoneyard adjoins the Old Road.

ARIZONA HISTORIC ROUTE 66
ASSOCIATION

The decommissioning of Route 66, completed in 1984, was a potentially devastating blow to the communities served by the Old Road. There were fears that livelihoods would disappear, and that the existence of entire towns and villages might be threatened. Citizens throughout the eight affected states began to form associations and pressure groups to preserve their way of life and keep 66 alive; and among the most successful of these was the Historic Route 66 Association of Arizona, led by longtime Seligman resident Angel Delgadillo, and Jerry Richard and David Wesson of Kingman. One of the Association's aims (realized within months of its formation in February 1987) was to have the section of highway from Seligman to Kingman officially declared "Historic Route 66," and properly signposted; this "Historic" designation was later extended to the entire surviving stretch of 66 in Arizona. Since then, the Association has established an impressive museum and gift shop at Kingman's Powerhouse Visitor Center, and it remains tireless in its promotion of the Mother Road throughout the region.

157

Above and top: Approaching Grand Canyon Caverns. The central reservation runs for only a short distance on this part of 66; the sign for the caverns themselves – an attraction since the 1920s – is on the left.

The Grand Canyon Caverns, whose entrance is about 24 miles (39km) northwest of Seligman, are a perennially popular place on this part of the highway; they have been described by Bob Moore and Patrick Grauwels as "a Roadie attraction that keeps on going despite the moving of the Road." These limestone caves – once part of a prehistoric seabed, but now dry and lifeless – were discovered in 1927, after heavy rain had widened an opening leading down to them. Comprising two vast main "rooms" and several other subterranean chambers, they attract over 70,000 visitors annually.

Nine miles (14km) beyond the Caverns is the settlement of Peach Springs, tribal capital for the Hualapai Native Americans who have lived along the banks of the Colorado River for the last 1500 years. 66 continues southwest, winding its way down Crozier Canyon in the footsteps of Lieutenant Edward Fitzgerald Beale, who led a trail-blazing expedition (accompanied by mules, horses, and camels) through this region in 1857. Beale gave his grandfather's name, Truxton, to an area near what is now Valentine, about 17 miles (27km) from Peach Springs. Here, in 1900, a brick-built school was

Above and top: These vivid Native American paintings decorate the walls of a disused kiosk close to the road near the Old Truxton Indian School.

opened for Native American children; its structure still survives, although the school itself has been closed for many years. In 1951, a new "Truxton" was constructed several miles closer to Peach Springs, as part of a subsequently abandoned plan for a railroad service to the Grand Canyon.

This section of highway (some of it unconcreted until the late 1930s) provides a taste of the sort of driving conditions that were typical in the days before the dull uniformity of most modern Interstates. More nostalgia for the Old Road can be found at Hackberry – whose General Store and Route 66 Visitor Center are featured in detail on the next two pages.

Right: A Brahman bull gazes impassively at passing traffic from a roadside field between Seligman and Grand Canyon Caverns.

Below: The Old Truxton Indian School near Valentine, established in 1900. Its historic buildings are now fenced off and boarded up.

Route 66 Visitor Center

Below: A Tokheim "Moneymaker" gas pump on display at the Hackberry Visitor Center. Pumps like these, showing both the amount of fuel delivered and its cost, first appeared on filling station forecourts and kerbs during the late 1930s.

The Old Hackberry Store, as it was originally known, dates from the 1930s; it did good business selling groceries and gas to travelers until the section of Route 66 passing through this area was bypassed by I-40 in 1978. Two years later, the store's owner, Tom Hill,

sold up; and after an abortive attempt to reopen the building as a dance bar in the late 1980s, it remained empty and abandoned until 1993, when it was purchased by artist and 66 expert Bob Waldmire (see pages 28-29).

In the months following his arrival at the store in October 1993, Bob created what he described as an "International-Bioregional Old Route 66 Visitor Center" there, as Tom Teague described in *Route 66 Magazine*: "In the depressions where the gas pumps used to be, he planted a cactus garden. On the south side of the main building, he built a solar greenhouse...Inside...tables and racks held his postcards, maps and posters. One corner held his father's book collection...in another corner, visitors could enjoy a cup of fresh coffee at an original Cozy Dog booth." The Visitor Center was soon attracting 100 or more visitors a day. However, Bob eventually became restless and unhappy living and working on site; he explained to Teague that "I [was] angry and tense and just resentful of how many people were going back and forth."

In October 1998, Bob left Hackberry to return to his native Illinois. Soon afterwards, the Visitor Center was sold to its present proprietors, John and Kerry Pritchard, who have continued to develop and enhance it – although the emphasis is now on Route 66 memorabilia rather than Bob's ecological concerns. Its many fascinating exhibits include a vintage Chevolet Corvette, and a display of gas pumps, signs, and other artifacts associated with the Old Road.

Right: Hackberry's Route 66 Visitor Center and General Store.

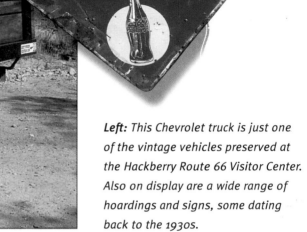

Left: This Chevrolet truck is just one of the vintage vehicles preserved at the Hackberry Route 66 Visitor Center. Also on display are a wide range of hoardings and signs, some dating back to the 1930s.

Far right: A burro *by the sidewalk in Oatman. These semi-wild donkeys mingle with the traffic in the old town.*
***Below:** The Sitgreaves Pass in pre-Route 66 days – a hair-raising drive for the vehicles of the time.*

ON THE NATIONAL OLD TRAILS HIGHWAY – OCEAN TO OCEAN

HAIR-PIN CURVE, NATIONAL OLD TRAILS HIGHWAY, BETWEEN KINGMAN AND OATMAN, ARIZONA

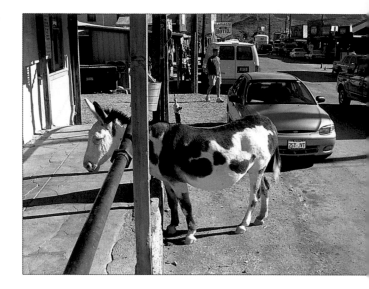

"Soon after leaving Hackberry," wrote Jack D. Rittenhouse in his 1946 guide, "you leave Crozier Canyon and wind out onto a great plain, on which the road runs amazingly straight into Kingman." The city dates from 1883, and we enter it on Andy Devine Boulevard – named for its most celebrated citizen, an actor famous for his "good guy" roles in movies and on TV. Devine's boyhood home was the Beale Hotel on what is now Andy Devine Avenue, and his career is documented in the Mohave Museum of History and Arts on West Beale Street. Another significant downtown attraction is the

> " What do we want with this worthless area, this region of savages and wild beasts, of shifting sands and whirlwinds of dust, of cactus and prairie dogs? To what use could we ever hope to put these great deserts and these endless mountain ranges? "

U.S. Secretary of State Daniel Webster, speaking about the West in 1852

Below: The Oatman Hotel – famous guests include Clark Gable and Carole Lombard, who spent their wedding night here in 1939.

Historic Route 66 Association of Arizona's Powerhouse Visitor Center, further details of which can be found on pages 188-189.

West of Kingman, we pass across the Sacramento Valley, a wide desert plain beyond which lie the Black Mountains and the notorious Gold Hill grade through the Sitgreaves Pass. It begins deceptively gently, but soon the gradient increases as the road winds around the mountainside. In nine miles (14km), we climb 1400 feet (425m), reaching a peak of 3515 feet (1071m) above sea level at the top of the pass, before making a precipitous descent into Oatman. This section of road can be demanding even for modern vehicles in good weather; traveling it in a more primitive automobile must have been a severe test of any driver's skill and nerves.

Oatman, once a mining community, retains some picturesque old buildings, although it is often overrun by tourists and traffic, and the *burros* (semi-wild donkeys) roaming its streets add to the congestion. 66 forms the town's main drag before continuing south. After about two miles (3km), bear left at the Y intersection to reach Golden Shores and Topock; here 66 rejoins I-40, and crosses the Colorado River into California.

Above left and right: The road through the Sacramento Valley culminates in a long, winding climb towards the top of the Sitgreaves Pass. This ascent, with its frequent hairpin bends, provides spectacular views of the surrounding terrain.

California

ROUTE 66

The vast expanse of the Mojave Desert is not as daunting to modern vehicles as it was to Steinbeck's Joad family – or to Jack Rittenhouse, who advised his readers to drive across it "either in the evening, night or early morning hours." But after the miles of scrub and dust, many travelers will relish the gentler, greener climate they encounter beyond the Cajon Pass, en route to 66's final destination: Santa Monica.

*Above: The Summit Inn Café at Cajon Summit offers travelers a last chance for refreshment before they head down the nearby pass to San Bernadino, 3000 feet (915m) below. **Main picture:** The desolate landscape of the Mojave Desert in Southern California.*

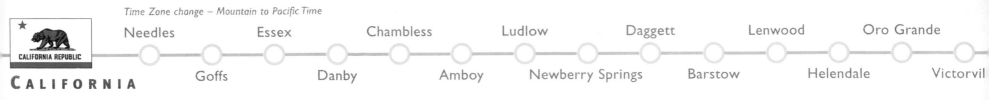
California

Below: *So much more than a road… as this souvenir "license plate" demonstrates, Route 66 has taken on an almost iconic significance - thanks in part to its portrayal by songwriter Bobby Troup and novelist John Steinbeck.*

The Mojave Desert is a formidable natural barrier, and passing through it is an adventure for all travelers, real and fictional. Sweet Betsy from Pike "gave out" and "lay rollin' about" in its sands; in *The Grapes of Wrath* the Joads headed through the Mojave after sundown to avoid "[getting] the livin' Jesus burned outa us"; while Raoul Duke and Doctor Gonzo, taking an alternative route (in more ways than one) from Los Angeles to Nevada in Hunter S. Thompson's *Fear and Loathing in Las Vegas*, had their own, highly illegal methods of coping with the rigors of the road.

Before trains and highways, this was a journey for only the hardiest and most committed. The first white man known to have completed it was Francisco Hermenegildo Garces, who traveled from Mexico via Needles to Oro Grande and San Bernadino in 1776. During the 19th century, Jedediah Smith (see pages 174-5 and 180-81), Mormon missionaries and Gold Rush prospectors were among the other pioneers to cross the region from the north. By the 1880s, the Colorado River had been bridged, and railroads were being built in the desert; a little later, as Michael Wallis explains, a section of the Old Trails Highway "developed out of a dirt track and a wooden plank trail that ran near the train tracks" from Needles. Its path was subsequently followed by Route 66 through much of California.

Staying close to the railroad took the highway north via Goffs, and in 1931, a more direct east-west road from Needles to Essex was introduced. This was the only substantial change ever made to the alignment of Route 66 in California, whose 320 miles (515km) were paved by the mid-1930s. Most

U.S. ROUTE 66 was christened in 1926. It started at Grant Park in Chicago, reached across more than 2,400 miles, three time zones and eight states - ILLINOIS, MISSOURI, KANSAS, OKLAHOMA, TEXAS, NEW MEXICO, ARIZONA and CALIFORNIA - before it dead-ended at Santa Monica Boulevard and Ocean Avenue in Santa Monica. It was the country's first two-lane road linking the shores of Lake Michigan and the Pacific Ocean. It was Bobby Troup's "GET YOUR KICKS ON ROUTE 66", a song that became a state of mind. Because it went through the center of so many towns, it became the "MAIN STREET OF AMERICA". John Steinbeck called it **"The Mother Road"**

McDonald's OVER 1 MILLION SOLD

Dick and Mac McDonald opened the world's first McDonald's Self-Service, Drive-In Restaurant on this site in San Bernardino, California December, 1948.

They previously operated a successful Drive-In Barbeque Restaurant with Carhop Service on this site from 1940 to 1948

Left: *A plaque at 14th and E. in San Bernadino marks the site of the first McDonald's.*

Below: *The Summit Inn at the top of the Cajon Pass dates from 1952.*

SUMMIT INN   SUMMIT INN CAFE

of the stretch between the Arizona border and Victorville is still driveable today, but beyond here, almost all the original highway has either been built over, or transformed by urbanization. However, a number of old motels, diners, and other buildings still survive, and San Bernadino and Pasadena have retained their interest and character.

Even in 1947, Jack D. Rittenhouse chose not to describe the road in detail beyond Pasadena; and today, there is little that is distinctive or charming about the congested maze of highways that lead through Hollywood to Santa Monica – although the magic of 66 reasserts itself as the road reaches its destination.

Right: Looking back up part of the old Cajon Pass alignment of 66 beyond the Cleghorn exit on I-15.

Left: Twilight at Santa Monica's Yacht Harbor, just beyond the end of Route 66

Below: 66's "finishing post" at Ocean Avenue and Santa Monica Boulevard.

Below: In the early days of 66, drivers, many of whom could not afford hotel accommodation, would often sleep in tents by the roadside – a practice that these 1930s Needles residents are determined to prevent!

For travelers expecting California to be a "sugar bowl" or a "Garden of Eden" (in the words of Woody Guthrie's *Do Re Mi*), the stony landscape on the western banks of the Colorado River must have been a harsh disappointment. This "broken rock wilderness" (as John Steinbeck called it in The *Grapes of Wrath*) has changed little since the 1930s, and there are still inspection stations on the road here, as there were in Steinbeck's novel and Guthrie's song. However, these are no longer concerned with Dust Bowl migrants, but only with animals, fruit, and vegetables coming across the state line, which also marks the boundary between the USA's Mountain and Pacific time zones.

Needles, about 12 miles (19km) from the border, was founded in 1883, after the completion of a railroad bridge across the Colorado; however, the river's strong currents swept away this crossing and

several of its successors, and there was no highway bridge here until 1916. The surrounding area remained subject to severe annual flooding until the Colorado was finally tamed by extensive damming and dredging in the 1950s.

After entering Needles and driving down Broadway (the old mule train wagon in the photograph above can be seen at its eastern end), rejoin I-40 at exit 141, and stay on the Interstate until exit 133. At this point, take US 95 north for about six miles (9km), and then make a left turn onto the Goffs Road. Goffs itself lies about 12 miles (19km) to the west; as we head towards it, the Santa Fe railroad runs close to the highway. Its massive trains – some over a mile long – are sometimes the only sign of life on this especially desolate section of the Old Road, which was bypassed by later, more direct alignments between Needles and Essex as early as 1931.

"Oh, if you ain't got the Do-Re-Mi, folks
If you ain't got the Do-Re-Mi
Why, you better go back to beautiful Texas
Oklahoma, Kansas, Georgia, Tennessee
California is a garden of Eden
A paradise to live in or see
But believe it or not you won't find it so hot
If you ain't got the Do-Re-Mi."

from "Do-Re-Mi" by Woody Guthrie, 1912–1967

*Above **and below**: A mule train wagon on display at Needles' A Street and Broadway. Before the advent of Route 66, primitive vehicles like this were the main form of freight transport in use on the region's rough, unsurfaced tracks.*

Needles Bridge.   Needles, Cal.

Above: The old highway bridge across the Colorado River – the gateway to California for countless travelers on Route 66.

Left: *Two freight trains passing near Goffs. The railroad carries massive loads like these across the desert en route to the port of San Diego.*

169

Right: 66 *en route to Amboy, seen from a rocky hillside above the road.*

Below: The view west from Goffs Road. Highway and railroad run close together for many miles in this area, and the monotony of the landscape is broken only by occasional isolated clusters of buildings.

After driving over the railroad tracks at Goffs, turn left and head south for about ten miles (16km), where the road crosses I-40 and leads southwest to Essex. The places marked on the map around here are often little more than isolated clusters of houses; Essex itself has a population of less than 100. In the next 35 miles (56km) we pass other tiny settlements, assigned a sequence of arbitrarily chosen, alphabetically ordered names by the Santa Fe company when it built its lines across the desert. Beyond Essex come Danby, Chambless, the site of Bristol (now vanished, although Bristol

Dry Lake lies to the south), and then Amboy – whose recently renovated appearance stands out sharply from its dusty surroundings. The settlement dates from the 1930s; its ten buildings, including Roy's Café and Motel, were purchased from their previous owner, Buster Burris, by Walt Wilson and Tim White in 1995, and extensively refurbished – Roy's now even boasts a gift shop!

Just south of the road beyond Amboy is an extinct volcano crater, named after the town – one of the few landmarks on our journey through the desert towards Ludlow, 28 miles (45km) away. This was once mining country, as Jack D. Rittenhouse

Right: A battered sign for a long-vanished roadside business. Ludlow still offers gas and refreshments to interstate travelers, but bears little trace of its former prosperity.

Below and inset below: The boarded-up Ludlow Café and an adjacent disused gas station on the largely abandoned west side of town.

explains in his guide to Route 66: "Between 1875 and 1910 the mountains of the Mojave were extensively exploited for…copper, silver, borax, gold and other minerals." At Ludlow, the ore from these workings was transferred to the main railroad line, and today, visitors to the town might still, as Bob Butcher put it in *Route 66 Magazine*, "hear the ghosts of hard rock miners… swapping tall tales over the lunch counter." We now cross I-40, spending a few miles on its north side before recrossing it at Lavic Road, and continuing to Newberry Springs, location for the 1988 movie *Bagdad Café*.

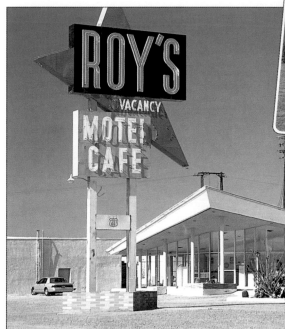

Left: Roy's Motel and Café, Amboy, smartly restored by Walt Wilson and Tim White, who own all the buildings in this tiny desert town.

171

Chevrolet Corvette

ROUTE 66

Above: The badge from the Corvette's hood – with a checkered racing flag and Chevrolet's distinctive emblem.

The Chevrolet Corvette, launched in 1953, was unlike any other American sports car. In fact, its inspiration came from the British market; General Motors design supremo Harley Earl and his colleagues conceived it as a competitor to the fast, sexy roadsters made by UK manufacturers like Jaguar, MG and Austin-Healey. Another factor that set the Corvette apart was its unique glassfiber body – although this feature was a constant problem for owners, who found that it leaked water and let in dust. There were also complaints about the Corvette's sluggish performance and indifferent handling; GM later responded to these by replacing the original six-cylinder engine with a new V8 unit, reshaping the body and offering manual transmission. Despite its early shortcomings, the 'vette's futuristic image quickly brought it cult status – and its appearance in the 1960–64 CBS TV show *route 66* (co-sponsored by Chevrolet and starring George Maharis and Martin Milner) must have sold more cars than any commercial. It has also inspired a clutch of classic pop songs – from *'54 Corvette* by The Customs (1963) to Prince's memorable 1983 hit *Little Red Corvette*.

This Corvette dates from the post-1958 era: among the distinctive features introduced in that year were the quadruple headlights and sidescooped front wings seen here.

The six-cylinder engine fitted to early Corvettes was replaced in 1955 by a 265cid V8 unit; two years later, there was a further increase in capacity, to 283cid.

CENTRAL & WESTERN UNITED STATES

Mobil

Mobil Service

Mobil Premium

Mobil

The original 1953 Corvette featured protruding "jet-pod" rear lights designed by General Motors' Harley Earl (who was also responsible for Cadillac's famous tailfins). By 1958, the Corvette had acquired a more smoothly shaped tail end.

The Chevrolet Corvette was never intended to be a big-production automobile: from 1953 to 1962 a total of just under 69,000 were made at the General Motors plants in St. Louis, Missouri and Flint, Michigan.

Just west of Newberry Springs, we cross again to the northern side of I-40, which runs almost parallel to 66. From here, it is about 11 miles (18km) to Daggett, where locally mined ore was once smelted before being shipped out via the two major railroad lines (the Santa Fe and Union Pacific) passing through the town. Daggett was also the site of two pioneering solar power plants operated by the Edison company, but dismantled in the late 1990s. We now take the Interstate to Barstow, where I-40 (which runs all the way from here to North Carolina) terminates at its junction with I-15, the main road south to San Diego.

Barstow developed from a settlement on the banks of the Mojave River providing supplies for

Above: The California Highway Patrol was created in 1929 to enforce traffic law throughout the state; these CHP officers were photographed in Barstow that same year. The Patrol expanded rapidly, boasting over 700 members by 1939, and later merged with the California State Police.

in honor of William Barstow Strong, ex-President of the Santa Fe Company. Today, Barstow lies slightly south of its original 19th century location; Route 66 passes through its Main Street.

Unlike some earlier travelers, who would leave the Old Road at this point and continue west to Bakersfield (whose rich farmlands provided grape- and fruit-picking work for many Dustbowl refugees) we stay on 66 as it follows the course of the river southwest towards Lenwood, Helendale, and Oro Grande. The level of the land begins to rise noticeably here – from 2106 feet (642m) at Barstow to 2631 feet (802m) at Oro Grande, where 66 crosses the river on the vintage steel bridge shown in the photograph.

Top: A highway marker at Helendale, on the road from Barstow to Victorville. Above: Barstow's historic railroad depot, which was also the site of a luxurious Harvey House hotel, the "Casa del Desierto."

traders, explorers, gold seekers, and other travelers making their way across the desert. In 1886, when it was still known as Waterman, it became the junction between the main east-west railroad and the newly-built Atchison, Topeka & Santa Fe line through the Cajon Pass; later that year, it was renamed Barstow

Above: A photo of the truss-type road bridge across the Mojave River at Oro Grande, taken during the early 1930s.

Right: The Bagdad Café, Newberry Springs – originally called the Sidewinder, it was renamed after Percy Adlon's eponymous movie was shot there.

175

Above: This Victorville museum celebrates Roy Rogers and his wife Dale Evans - co-stars in countless Westerns.

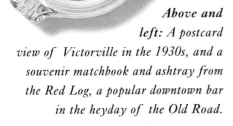

Above and left: A postcard view of Victorville in the 1930s, and a souvenir matchbook and ashtray from the Red Log, a popular downtown bar in the heyday of the Old Road.

Victorville, named for Jacob Nash Victor, who oversaw the construction of the AT&SF railroad line through this area, was founded in 1885. Originally a mining community, it went on to find favor with Hollywood producers as a movie location, particularly for Westerns. One of the stars who shot his pictures here was Roy Rogers (1911–1998), and the museum on Seneca Road devoted to his life and work attracts thousands of visitors every year (see pages 188–189).

Another important local attraction, the California Route 66 Museum, lies just one block from the path of the Old Road through Victorville; after crossing the Oro Grande bridge, head under I-15 to D Street, and turn right onto 6th to reach it. Among the many fascinating items on display are relics from "Hulaville" – the collection of strange signs, wine bottle "trees," and other bizarre items that once stood about five miles (8km) out of town. Created by ex-carnival showman Miles Mahan (1896–1997), the site was a famous landmark on 66 for many years.

Leaving Victorville, take 7th Street to its junction with I-15, and rejoin the Interstate as it climbs towards Cajon Summit, about 18 miles (29km) to the southwest. Little of Route 66 remains here, although it is possible to use a surviving stretch of highway during our descent through the Cajon Pass to San Bernadino; see the next two pages for a detailed description of this section of road.

At the bottom of the pass, stay on Cajon Boulevard, continue underneath Highland Avenue, and then join Mount Vernon Avenue. From here, a right turn onto Foothill Boulevard puts us on the path of Old 66 for the final stretch of our journey; nearby are the site of the first ever McDonald's Restaurant, dating from 1948, and the lovely old California Theater at 562 West 4th Street.

Above: Part of a surviving stretch of Route 66 leading down toward San Bernadino. Although two of its lanes have now been closed to traffic, this alignment gives some idea of what the Old Road through the Cajon Pass might have been like.

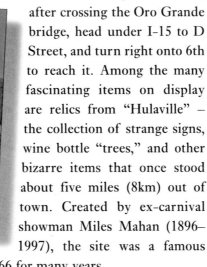

***Right:** The original McDonald's in San Bernadino. The McDonald Brothers' "Speedee Service System," introduced here in 1948 (when burgers were 15¢ and fries just a dime) went on to revolutionize the fast food business worldwide.*

HULAVILLE

Miles Marion Mahan was born on June 9, 1896 in Phoenix, Arizona, and spent much of his life working for carnivals and traveling circuses. While attending a rodeo at Victorville in 1955, he took a fancy to a half-acre parcel of desert land sited south of town on Amargosa Road, adjacent to Route 66. He bought it, set up home there in a camper truck, and started to surround himself with the strange jumble of salvaged "treasures," painted signs (some of them memorials to his long-dead carny buddies) and other odd artifacts that became known as Hulaville. The collection took its name from a 12-foot high metal "hula girl" billboard, purchased from a scrap heap for a dollar and erected to attract passing motorists.

Mahan ran his roadside museum until 1995, and died two years later, aged 100. Much of Hulaville's contents (including the hula girl sign) can now be seen at Victorville's California Route 66 Museum, which also features a superbly detailed diorama of the original site made by local craftsman Steve Anderson.

Painted signs from Hulaville, created by Miles Mahan and now preserved in Victorville's Route 66 Museum.

Cajon Summit & Pass

Below: *The Summit Inn Café at the top of the Cajon Pass – a Route 66 institution offering food and drinks for every taste. The Old Road ran directly past the café, from where it was once possible to see the faces of travelers driving by in their cars.*

Cajon Summit stands 4260 feet (1299m) above sea level; here the road begins its descent through a cleft in the mountains to San Bernadino, over 3000 feet (915m) below. To the left of I-15, near the Oak Hill exit, lies the Summit Inn, opened in 1952 to cater for travelers seeking refreshment – and, perhaps, wishing to steady their nerves – before this ordeal. The Summit still offers excellent food (including ostrich burgers!); adjacent to it is a long-established Texaco gas station, with a group of vintage trucks parked nearby.

Jack D. Rittenhouse described the old highway through the Cajon Pass as "a great descending sweep," advising drivers to use second gear for safety, and commenting on "the wonderful, changing vistas of green valleys and mountain ranges in various shades of blue." The modern route is still exhilarating, but less dramatic, although a surviving stretch of 66 on the way down provides a taste of how things once were. To reach it, leave I-15 at the Cleghorn Road exit and follow Cajon Boulevard; this six-mile (9km) alignment

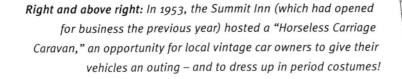

***Right and above right:** In 1953, the Summit Inn (which had opened for business the previous year) hosted a "Horseless Carriage Caravan," an opportunity for local vintage car owners to give their vehicles an outing – and to dress up in period costumes!*

includes a section divided into four lanes (although only two are now in use), and eventually comes to a dead end just west of the Kenwood Avenue intersection with I-15. Rejoin the freeway here, but prepare to exit onto I-215 soon afterwards, at the point where 15 turns away to the south.

A short distance from here, turn off I-215 at Devore Road, rejoin Cajon Boulevard, and continue through Devore itself and on towards San Bernadino. The rich, lush valley we are now entering is a welcome contrast to the desert landscape that has dominated so much of Route 66's journey through California; we finally seem to have reached the "Promised Land" that so many migrants dreamed of finding here.

This page: Gas station artifacts at the Cajon Summit site: a Tokheim portable gas pump designed in the 1900s; a horse-drawn gas wagon originally used by street vendors; and a more modern tanker truck.

As we head down Foothill Boulevard, we already seem to be in suburban Los Angeles – there is little relief from urban sprawl, traffic, and smog in the remaining 70 miles (113km) that separate us from our destination. Nevertheless, the communities we pass through manage to retain some individuality, and the route is dotted with interesting sites and places dating from the days before the big city encroached into this area.

One of the most distinctive of these is the Wigwam Motel in Rialto, near the intersection with Pepper Street, about four miles (6km) from where we turned onto Foothill. The Wigwam – whose teepees offer color TV and air-conditioning – opened in 1950, making it almost exactly contemporary with the Wigwam Village in Holbrook, Arizona (see pages 146–147). A little further west lies the town of Fontana, and Bono's

Above and top: The Wigwam Motel, 2728 W. Foothill Boulevard. Sadly, the sign once displayed outside the premises inviting potential guests to "do it in a tee pee" has now been removed!

Right: The Virginia Dare Winery, Rancho Cucamonga. This building, once owned by the Garrett wine-making firm, dates from 1910.

Rancho Cucamonga | 2243 | Claremont | 2247 | Glendora | 2255 | Duarte | 2259 | Arcadia
2240 | Upland | 2245 | La Verne | 2252 | Azusa | 2257 | Monrovia | 2261

Right: The Madonna of the Trail: one of 12 statues erected in the 1920s by the Daughters of the American Revolution to commemorate the achievements of the nation's "pioneer mothers."

Above: Good eats in traditional Route 66 style: Bono's in Fontana has been serving hungry travelers on Foothill Boulevard for over 60 years.

Restaurant and Deli: another Route 66 institution, managed by the same Italian–American family since 1936, when there was still an abundance of vineyards and citrus groves in the region. Rancho Cucamonga, roughly ten miles (16km) beyond Fontana, was the site of the first winery in California, dating from 1839; a later winery building, the Virginia Dare, now serves as a shopping mall.

Next is Upland, whose "Madonna of the Trail" statue, dedicated in 1929 and showing a pioneer woman clutching a baby in her arms while holding a rifle in her right hand, commemorates the Western USA's early migrant settlers, and provides a reminder of this stretch of highway's rich history. As the plaque on the statue's pedestal explains, the road was originally a trail "trod by the padres in Spanish days," and also the path taken by Jedediah Smith (1799–1831) – the explorer who, in November 1826, led the first group of white Americans into what became the state of California.

Drive-ins

Opposite page: Two flourishing Old Road ozoners – the 66 Drive-In (Carthage, MO) with its special FM sound system (inset sign); and the Frisina Sky View near Litchfield, IL. Both venues are closed during the winter.

Below: The Foothill Drive-In, 675 East Foothill Boulevard, Azusa, CA, opened in 1955, and is the state's largest surviving solo-screen ozoner.

In August 6, 1932, Richard M. Hollingshead, Jr. of Riverton, New Jersey, submitted a patent application for his new invention – a drive-in cinema, using a system of ramps that allowed people to sit in cars and watch movies without having their view obscured by other vehicles. The patent was granted the following May, and on June 6, 1933, the nearby town of Camden was the venue for Hollingshead's first-ever drive-in film presentation. Admission cost 25¢, the featured picture was *Wife Beware*, starring Adolph Menjou, and the show was a sell-out.

Over the next few years, nearly 100 more "ozoners" (the nickname refers to the theaters' roofless, open-air design) opened throughout the USA. Their spread slowed during World War II; but after 1945, numbers of drive-ins rose faster than ever, reaching a peak of nearly 5000 during their greatest boom period: the 1950s.

Although facilities and layouts varied, with some drive-ins offering additional attractions such as playgrounds, animal shows, and even boat rides, the basic viewing experience was much the same whatever the size and sophistication of the theater.

66 DRIVE-IN THEATRE
CARTHAGE, MO.

66 DRIVE-IN
NOW SHOWING
CLOSED
359-5959

106.5 STEREOPHONIC F M SOUND
Please TURN OFF YOUR HEADLAMPS
NO ALCOHOLIC BEVERAGES

DRIVE IN
Frisina SKY VIEW Theatre
CLOSED FOR THE SEASON
VISIT OUR SNACK BAR

Customers shared the collective thrill of watching a film, but did so in the privacy of their cars, where they could behave as they pleased without disturbing – or being observed by – other people. Unsurprisingly, a substantial proportion of most audiences was made up of couples who were more interested in each other than in what was happening on screen!

Ozoners' popularity suffered a steep decline from the late 1960s onwards, and most of the theaters that once flourished along Route 66 could not survive the fatal combination of falling audiences and the decommissioning of the highway itself. A few remain open for business; up to date news and information about them can be found in *Route 66 Magazine*, and also on a specialist website, www.driveinmovie.com.

Below: Monrovia's Aztec Hotel, built in 1925. This remarkable building, combining Art Deco with Mayan and Aztec influences, was restored in 1983, and is now on the National Register of Historic Places.

Bottom: The Stardust Motel, near Foothill and Cerritos, in Azusa.

Route 66, continuing down Foothill Boulevard, now enters Los Angeles County and the city of Claremont, developed in 1887 on land that was formerly part of the vast Mission San Gabriel Arcángel (built just south of Pasadena in the late 18th century), and incorporated in 1907. After heading through La Verne, the road passes underneath I-210 en route for Glendora, where, for a short stretch, we move onto Alosta Avenue before rejoining Foothill at the intersection with Citrus.

Next, we come to Azusa, given its name by early ranchers, and laid out at about the same time as Claremont. At 675 E. Foothill is the Foothill Drive-In Theatre, a thriving single-screen cinema dating from the 1950s.

Just west of here we pass Azusa's Stardust Hotel, with its classic "retro" styling; a few miles later, we cross the San Gabriel River, and Foothill becomes Huntingdon Drive as we reach Duarte. In his essay *Huntington Drive – Highway of History*, local historian Steve Baker paints a fascinating picture of this area in the early days of Route 66, when "orange groves abounded on both sides of the highway" and there was still only a handful of roadside businesses. Every year, the town of Duarte commemorates aspects of the Old

Above: Route 66 in Duarte: looking west down Huntington Boulevard at the intersection with Swiss Trails Road.

Road's past in its Route 66 street parades, which incorporate classic cars, historical costumes, and other 'period' attractions.

Monrovia, about two miles (3km) west of Duarte, was founded in 1886 by William N. Monroe, owner of a nearby ranch. Its most notable building, the Aztec Hotel, dates from 1925, and is located a little north of Huntington Drive, at 311 W. Foothill (between Magnolia Avenue and Alta Vista). Created by architect Robert Stacy-Judd (1884– 1975), the Aztec combines Art Deco and Latin American influences, and features a Mayan-style mural by Stacy-Judd's wife in its lobby.

2247	Glendora	2255	Duarte	2259	Arcadia	2269	Hollywood	2297
La Verne	2252	Azusa	2257	Monrovia	2261	Pasadena	2280	Santa Monica

· VOICE OF THE ROAD ·

Bobby Troup

In 1946, Nat King Cole recorded one of his biggest-ever hits: "(Get Your Kicks On) Route 66." Its composer, Bobby Troup (1918–1999), had enjoyed pre-war success in his native Pennsylvania with songs for Sammy Kaye and Tommy Dorsey; but after five years' military service, he was seeking a change of scene, as he explained in 1995 to writer Eliot Tiegel. "I told my mother there were two places to go as a songwriter, New York and the West Coast. I liked the West Coast and I was going to give myself two years to see if I could write songs [there]." En route to LA, Troup sketched out some lyrics inspired by his journey on 66, and was thrilled when Cole – "my idol" – took up the completed number. It has since become an established classic.

Troup himself, who subsequently achieved fame and fortune as a Hollywood-based musician and actor, described it as "a sort of theme song about the 'Main Street of America'."

Left: Route 66 runs along Foothill for much of its journey from San Bernadino to Pasadena near Los Angeles.

Above: Bobby Troup (third from left) pictured in 1998 at his home in LA with members of the British group The Quest.

Right: The art deco Georgian Hotel, on Santa Monica's Ocean Avenue, dates from 1933, and has played host to countless Hollywood stars.

Below: Route 66 as it once was in this area; west of Pasadena, almost all traces of the Old Road have vanished beneath newer highway systems.

Above: Pasadena's elegantly arched Colorado Street Bridge, built in 1912.

Huntington Drive leads us westward from Monrovia to Arcadia; here we take Colorado Boulevard into Pasadena, where drivers willing to delay their arrival in Los Angeles may choose to linger a little. Like Claremont and several other surrounding settlements, the town developed around the nearby San Gabriel Arcángel Mission (see pages 184-185). Its many historic buildings include the Playhouse on El Molino Avenue, built in 1917; the grand mansions on Orange Grove Boulevard, among them properties once owned by David Gamble (of Proctor and Gamble) and chewing-gum magnate William Wrigley; and the classic Colorado Street Bridge over the Arroyo Seco.

Beyond Pasadena, the complexities of L.A.'s modern highway system soon obliterate any real sense of being on Route 66, although the approximate path of the Old Road to Santa Monica can be followed by entering Arroyo Parkway from Colorado Boulevard, continuing southwest on the Pasadena Freeway (State 110), exiting onto Figueroa Street, and then heading west on Sunset Boulevard before joining Santa Monica Boulevard.

This last stage of our journey takes us through the sometimes glamorous, but often seedy streets of Hollywood. By winding the car window down, we can inhale what one visitor to the city, opera singer Robert Tear, described in his autobiography *Tear Here* as "an odd arrangement of air, with the sweet-smelling flowers and the heady scent of pine-trees mixed with benzene." But as we approach the final few blocks before the intersection of Santa Monica and Ocean Boulevard, there is another ingredient: the sea breeze, which begins to freshen the atmosphere even before the Pacific itself comes into view. The meeting of the two roads marks the end of Route 66; all that now separates us from the water is Palisades Park, with its plaque marking the dedication of "the Main Street of America" to Will Rogers in 1952.

Above: A plaque in Palisades Park honors Will Rogers' links with Route 66.

Below: This colorful ferris wheel is just one of the many attractions of the funfair at Santa Monica pier.

"
Go West, young man, Go West. "

Horace Greeley (1811–1872)

Above: The waterfront and gateway to Santa Monica's Yacht Harbor lie just beyond Palisades Park, a short stroll from the highway.
Left: Santa Monica Boulevard and Ocean Avenue – the end of Route 66's long journey from Chicago.

Right: A vintage handbill for Pasadena's Tournament of Roses. The event, inaugurated in 1890 and featuring an elaborate parade of flower-decorated floats, takes place each New Year's Day

Resources & Bibliography

USEFUL ADDRESSES AND INTERNET LINKS

ROUTE 66 ORGANIZATIONS AND RESOURCES

Historic Route 66
Internet: route66.netvision.be/
This site is invaluable for route planning; it contains detailed driving directions for the entire length of the Old Road

Route 66 Magazine
326 West Route 66
Williams, AZ 86046
Internet:
www.route66magazine.com
E-mail:
info@route66magazine.com

Drive-In Movie Information
These two internet sites provide comprehensive, up to date information on Route 66's drive-in movie theaters:
www.driveinmovie.com
www.driveintheater.com/route66.htm

STATE-BY-STATE INFORMATION

ILLINOIS
Route 66 Association of Illinois
2743 Veterans Parkway #166
Springfield, IL 62704
Internet: www.i66assoc.org/

Funks Grove Pure Maple Sirup
(pages 24–25)
RR #1, Box 41A, Shirley, IL 61772

Dixie Truckers Home
(pages 26–27)
Junction I-55 & US 136,
Exit 145
McLean, Illinois
(Mailing Address:
P.O. Box 450
McLean, IL 61754)
Internet:
www.dixietruckershome.com/

Springfield Illinois Convention
& Visitors Bureau (pages 28–29)
109 North Seventh Street,
Springfield IL 62701
Internet:
www.springfield.il.us/visit

Abraham Lincoln website (links to various Springfield sites)
Internet:
www.starfirepro.com/lincoln.htm

Cozy Drive In & Supply Co.
(pages 28–29)
2935 South Sixth Street,
Springfield, IL 62703

MISSOURI
Route 66 Association of Missouri
P.O. Box 8117
St. Louis, MO 63156
Internet: www.missouri66.org

Old Chain Of Rocks Bridge
Group (pages 42–43)
Internet:
home.att.net/~old.chain.of.rocks.bridge/
E-mail: old.chain.of.rocks.bridge@worldnet.att.net

Meramec Caverns
(pages 44–45, 90–91)
I-44 West, Exit 230
Stanton, MO
Internet:
www.americascave.com/

KANSAS
Kansas Route 66 Association
P.O. Box 169
Riverton, KS 66770

OKLAHOMA
Oklahoma Route 66 Association
P.O. Box 21382
Oklahoma City, OK 73156
Internet:
oklahoma66.com

Will Rogers sites (pages 72–75)
Internet:
www.willrogers.org/

Round Barn, Arcadia
(pages 76–77)
The Old Round Barn,

P.O. Box 134,
Arcadia, OK 73007
Internet:
www.digitalmonkey.com/oldbarn/

National Cowboy Hall of Fame,
Oklahoma City (pages 78–79)
1700 NE 63rd Street
Oklahoma City, OK 73111
Internet:
www.cowboyhalloffame.org/

Oklahoma Historical Society
2100 N. Lincoln Boulevard
Oklahoma City, OK 73105
Internet:
www.ok-history.mus.ok.us/

Oklahoma Route 66 Museum
(pages 82–83)
2229 W. Gary Blvd.
Clinton, OK 73601
Internet: www.route66.org/

National Route 66 Museum
(pages 86–87)
P.O. Box 5
Elk City, OK 73648
Internet:
www.national66.com/elk_city/index.html

TEXAS
Old Route 66 Association of Texas
P.O. Box 66
McLean, TX 79057

Midpoint Café (pages 110–111)
Route 66, Adrian, TX 79001

Internet: us.worldpages.com/
806-538-6379/
E-mail: midpoint66@aol.com

NEW MEXICO
New Mexico Route 66
Association
1415 Central Avenue NE
Albuquerque, NM 81706
Internet: www.rt66nm.org/

Route 66 Diner
(pages 126-127)
1405 E. Central Avenue,
Albuquerque, NM 87106-4802
Internet: www.66diner.com/

ARIZONA
Historic Route 66 Association
of Arizona
P.O. Box 66
Kingman, AZ 86402
Internet: www.azrt66.com

Painted Desert/Petrified Forest
(pages 146-147)
P.O. Box 2217
Petrified Forest National Park,
AZ 86028
Internet:
www.desertusa.com/pet/index.
html

La Posada Hotel
(pages 152-153)
303 East 2nd Street, Historic
U.S. Route 66,
Winslow AZ 86047
Internet:
www.laposada.org
Email: laposada@igc.org

Old Route 66 Visitor Center &
General Store
 (pages 158-159)
Box 46, Hackberry, AZ 86411

CALIFORNIA
California Historic Route 66
Association
2127 Foothill Boulevard #66
La Verne, CA 91750
Internet:
wemweb.com/chr66a/index.html

The Roy Rogers-Dale Evans
Museum
(pages 176-177)
15650 Seneca Road, Victorville,
CA 92392
Internet: www.royrogers.com/

California Route 66 Museum
(pages 176-177)
P. O. Box 2151
Victorville, CA 92393.
Internet:
www.national66.com/victorville
/index.html

BIBLIOGRAPHY

Caughey, John Walton: *California* (Prentice-Hall, 1940)
Cooke, Alistair: *Alistair Cooke's America* (BBC, 1974)
Crump, Spencer: *Route 66 – America's First Main Street* (Zeta Publishers, 1996)
Freeth, Nick: *Traveling Route 66* (University of Oklahoma Press, 2001)

Guthrie, Woody: *Bound for Glory* (E.P. Dutton & Co, 1943)
Hamons, Lucille: *Lucille: Mother of the Mother Road* (Cheryl Hamons Nowka, 1997)
Kelly, Susan Croce & Scott, Quinta: *Route 66 – The Highway and its People* (University of Oklahoma Press, 1988)
Kerouac, Jack: *On The Road* (The Viking Press, 1957, current edition Viking Penguin)
Kirby, Doug, Smith, Ken, & Wilkins, Mike: *The New Roadside America* (Fireside/Simon & Schuster, 1992)
Kotkin, Joel & Grabowicz, Paul: *California Inc.* (Discus Books, 1983)
Mahnke, Dan: *Antique Roads of America, Bicycle Guide for Route 66* (Dan Mahnke, 1992)
Moore, Bob and Grauwels, Patrick: *Route 66 – The Illustrated Guidebook to the Mother Road* (Roadbook International, 1998)
Queener, S. Suzann: *Law and Disorder – Greene County's Notorious Past* (Greene County Archives & Records Center, 1999)
Repp, Thomas Arthur: *Route 66 – The Empires of Amusement* (Mock Turtle Press, 1999)
Rittenhouse, Jack D.: *A Guide Book to Highway 66* (University of New Mexico Press facsimile edition, 1989)

Snyder, Tom: *The Route 66 Traveler's Guide and Roadside Companion* (St. Martin's Press, New York, 1995)
Steinbeck, John: *The Grapes of Wrath* (pub.1939, current edition Viking Penguin)
Suttle, Howard: *Behind The Wheel…On Route 66* (Mass Market, 1996)
Thompson, Hunter S.: *Fear and Loathing in Las Vegas* (Straight Arrow Publisher Inc., 1971)
Waldmire, Bob: *A Nostalgic, Bioregionally-Flavored, Bird's-Eye-View Map of Old Route 66* (R. Waldmire, 1992)
Wallis, Michael: *Route 66: The Mother Road* (St. Martin's Press, New York, 1990)
Ward, Geoffrey C.: *The West: An Illustrated History* (Little Brown & Co., 1996)
Ward, Greg (ed.): *USA – The Rough Guide* (The Rough Guides, 1994)
Wheat, Carolyn (ed.): *Murder on Route 66* (Berkley Prime Crime Books, 1999)
Witzel, Michael Karl: *Route 66 Remembered* (Motorbooks International, 1996)

Index

I · N · D · E · X

Acknowledgements

The author would like to thank the many individuals and organizations who were so generous with their assistance and advice during the research and writing of this book. Especial thanks to Ron Adamson; Anne Baker (History Museum for Springfield-Greene County, Springfield, MO); Nan Elsasser, Executive Director, Working Classroom Inc., Albuquerque, NM; Mrs. Glaida Funk (Funks Grove, IL); Rodger Harris and the staff of the Oklahoma Historical Society, Oklahoma City; Fran Houser (Midpoint Café, Adrian, TX); Dan Harlow and Steve Anderson (Route 66 Museum, Victorville, CA); La Posada Foundation, Winslow, AZ; the staff at Bill Murphey's Route 66 Café, Baxter Springs, KS; Bob Moore; Kerry Pritchard (Old Route 66 Visitor Center & General Store, Hackberry, AZ); John Pugh; Larry Sleight; Pat Smith (Route 66 Museum, Clinton, OK); Paul, Sandi and Jessi Taylor; and Bob and Buz Waldmire.

Sincere thanks also to Neil Sutherland, who took all the original photos in the book, and did the driving on our journey down Route 66!

The Dorothea Lange photograph *Family on the Road, Oklahoma, 1938* (page 8) is reproduced by kind permission of the Oakland Museum of California.

The picture of Cadillac Ranch (© The Ant Farm) on page 107 is reproduced by kind permission of the copyright holders.

The Joe Stephenson mural *"The Mother Road"/"El Camino de los Caminos"* (© Working Classroom Inc. 1995) on page 129 is reproduced by kind permission of the copyright holder.

The photograph of *On The Corner* (page 152) shows a bronze by Ron Adamson and an adjacent mural by John Pugh. These are reproduced by kind permission of the artists and the La Posada Foundation, Winslow, AZ.

The Fran Houser quotations on pages 110–11 are taken from an article by Rick Storm published in the Amarillo Globe-News in August 1998, and are reproduced by kind permission of the newspaper.

The Bobby Troup quotation on page 185 is taken from Eliot Tiegel's liner notes for the CD *Kicks on 66* (© Hindsight Records Inc. 1995) and is reproduced by kind permission of the copyright holder.

The extract from *Route 66 – America's First Main Street* by Spencer Crump (© Spencer Crump 1994, 1996) on page 39 is reproduced by kind permission of the author and the publisher, Zeta Publishers Company.

The extracts from *Route 66 – The Highway and its People* by Susan Croce Kelly & Quinta Scott (© University of Oklahoma Press 1988) on pages 10, 26, 48–9, 68, and 91 are reproduced by kind permission of the copyright holder.

The extracts from *A Guide Book to Highway 66* by Jack D. Rittenhouse (© Jack D. Rittenhouse 1946, 1989) on pages 30, 46, 50, 60, 88–9, 93, 94, 105, 122, 133, 136, 162, 171 and 178 are reproduced by kind permission of the copyright holder and the publisher, University of New Mexico Press.

The extracts from *The Route 66 Traveler's Guide and Roadside Companion* by Tom Snyder (© Thomas J. Snyder 1990, 1995) on pages 57, 60, 83 and 152 are reproduced by kind permission of the author and the publisher, St. Martin's Press.

The extracts from Behind The Wheel…On Route 66 by Howard Suttle (© Howard Suttle 1993) on pages 94 and 112 are reproduced by kind permission of the author and the publisher, Data Plus! Printing and Publishing.

The extract from *Tear Here* by Robert Tear (© Robert Tear 1990) on page 186 is reproduced by kind permission of the author.

The extracts from *Route 66: The Mother Road* by Michael Wallis (© Michael Wallis 1990) on pages 84, 94 and 166 are reproduced by kind permission of the author and the publisher, St. Martin's Press.

The extract from *Route 66 Remembered* by Michael Karl Witzel (© Michael Witzel 1996) on page 22 is reproduced by kind permission of the author and the publisher, Motorbooks International.

The quotation on page 19 is from *"Route 66,"* words and music by Bobby Troup © London Town Music, Edwin H. Morris and Co Inc. and Burke & Van Heusen Inc., USA, Warner/Chappell Music Ltd, London W6 8BS, lyrics reproduced by permission of IMP Ltd. All rights reserved.

The quotation on page 81 is from *Incident on Sixth Street* by D.R. Meredith which appears in *Murder on Route 66*, edited by Carolyn Wheat (Berkley Publishing 1999), and is reproduced by permission of the author and copyright holder.

The quotations on pages 89 and 113 are from *The Grapes of Wrath* by John Steinbeck. Copyright © 1939, renewed © 1967 by John Steinbeck. Used by permission of Viking-Penguin, a division of Penguin Putnam Inc.

The quotation on page 105 is from *Bound For Glory* by Woody Guthrie. Copyright © 1943 by E.P. Dutton, renewed © 1971 by Marjorie M. Guthrie. Used by permission of Dutton, a division of Penguin Putnam Inc.

The quotation on page 119 is from *Rest Stop* by Lillian M. Roberts which appears in *Murder on Route 66*, edited by Carolyn Wheat (Berkley Publishing 1999), and is reproduced by permission of the author and copyright holder.

The quotation from page 169 is from *"Do Re Mi,"* words and music by Woody Guthrie © 1961 Ludlow Music Inc., New York, USA. Assigned to TRO Essex Music Ltd of Suite 2.07, Plaza 535 Kings Road, London SW10 0SZ. International copyright secured. All rights reserved. Used by permission.

Picture Credits